Strength
for All
Seasons

ALSO BY JULIE LAVENDER

Children's Bible Stories for Bedtime

Strength for All Seasons

A MOM'S DEVOTIONAL OF POWERFUL VERSES AND PRAYERS

JULIE LAVENDER

Zeitgeist • New York

To mommies and mom-figures all over the
world, in whatever fashion you earned that
title—God sees you and loves you. Treasure
and enjoy every season of motherhood!

Contents

Introduction

Motherhood.

Quite possibly the most treasured, yet most challenging, hat we wear. In whatever fashion you became a mom—biological children, bonus children from a blended marriage, foster kids and adopted kiddos, or children who adopted you as a mom figure—being a mom is an extraordinary gift from God.

God chose you to raise and care for those children—children he loves immeasurably more than you could ever imagine. He loves them (and YOU) so much that he wants to be with you and guide you on each step of the parenting journey.

God sees and understands your difficulties. The sacrifices you make. The huge responsibilities. The stress of bringing up children in a world that doesn't always recognize him as heavenly Father. The burnout from trying to raise the perfect family in a troubled world.

The heartaches and hardships are real!

Weary moms, God wants to strengthen you for the tough days. With a never-ending love, he wants to be your hope and salvation and support. He longs to comfort you on the hard days, encourage you when you face challenges, and inspire you to be the best mom you can be!

In *Strength for All Seasons*, you'll find devotions for moms of all stages, ages, and challenges. With cherry-picked verses to accompany 52 devotions, you'll wrap your heart securely around intentional, truth-bearing verses to help you overcome and thrive.

Beloved moms, you are never alone. God is just a whisper away. Keep this book close as you gather strength for the seasons of life and motherhood and find your way back to God.

He loves you so!

Perfectionism—An Unattainable Goal

For all have sinned and fall short of the glory of God.
ROMANS 3:23 (NIV)

A distant relative I admired, with her perfect marriage, perfect home, three perfect children, perfect career, and spot-on wardrobe, passed through town when my firstborn was 18 months old. Not on his best behavior at the restaurant, Jeremy didn't last long in the high chair.

He wiggled on the bench next to me and played with his food.

"I bet your kids never behaved like this," I faltered.

"They didn't," she said. "We taught our kids how to behave at the table."

Ouch. Could I ever match her perfection?

God doesn't expect perfect moms. In fact, he pointed out that we could never attain perfection in Romans 3:23. We will ALWAYS fall short.

Social media photos and posts often give a false image of "the perfect life" in someone else's home. Airbrushed celebrity photos in magazines and television shows contribute to the misconception that perfection is attainable. Striving to meet those standards damages our self-esteem and self-worth.

The truth is, God loves us despite our mistakes. His grace and mercy are so big that he wraps his arms around our mess-ups and covers our imperfections with his love. We don't have to be perfect because we are perfectly loved by the One who made us.

Oh, and the distant relative that I still admire? Years later, she walked away from an unhappy marriage, changed careers several times, and loves her imperfect children and grandchildren with great gusto.

REFLECTIONS

- In what specific areas do you strive for perfection? Body image? Relationships with other adults? Raising kids? Your profession? Church activities? Education? Appearance of your home? Sometimes the pursuit of perfection comes from unrealistic expectations imposed on us in childhood or young adulthood. Not always maliciously imposed, but there nonetheless. What can you tangibly do to forgive that person or persons who put undue pressure on you and move past those feelings?
- What unhealthy practices do you have that contribute to your desire for perfection? How can you limit or avoid those practices? Remember, the perfect mom or family or home doesn't exist, even when social media declares otherwise. Does scrolling or screen time add frustration and angst to your imperfect world?
- What can you do to embrace your imperfections? Do you laugh at your mess-ups? Do you learn from your mistakes? How do you persevere despite initial failures?

PRAYER

Dear God, when I bend toward perfectionism, help
me lean into you instead. Remind me that you love
me perfectly and unconditionally. Amen.

The Comparison Game—No One Wins

*Pay careful attention to your own work, for then you
will get the satisfaction of a job well done, and you
won't need to compare yourself to anyone else.*

GALATIANS 6:4 (NLT)

Edith stole a glance at the other moms. She knew *that* one—bright pink blouse, matching earrings, married to a pharmacist—bought clothes without looking at price tags. Meanwhile, cute-jumpsuit mom just finished a graduate degree while shuttling one child to dance lessons four days a week and one to travel baseball games every weekend.

Perky mom with perfect teeth just got a promotion, and the one sitting next to her successfully led two homeschool co-ops each week.

Edith pondered silently, "I'll bet their homes are immaculate, too, while I have spit-up on my sleeve, two hungry kids at home with the sitter, and unanswered emails waiting for me at work tomorrow."

Can you relate to Edith's comparison game?

We moms tend to compare ourselves to other moms. It's fairly common, but not healthy. It robs us of appreciating what we have and riddles us with envy for what someone else has. It steals our joy!

True contentment comes from a relationship with God. God made us just the way he wanted, to be the moms we are, for such a time as this. To compare ourselves to others implies God made a mistake when he made us. And God doesn't make mistakes! We are loved and treasured by our Maker. We are our Father's favorite, and let's not forget that!

- What makes it easy for you to slip into the comparison game? Aimlessly gazing at social media? Spending time with others whose conversations lean toward comparisons? A challenging day and not enough sleep? What can you do differently to avoid these situations?
- God picked you to be the mom of your kiddos, and no one can parent your child or children better than you. What words can you use to remind yourself each day to treasure your parenting journey and avoid comparing your parenting to that of others around you?
- What "work" do you need to pay attention to more closely so that you won't have time for comparisons? Did you cook a healthy, balanced meal tonight? Celebrate with dessert! Did you make time to play outside with the kids? Celebrate with lemonade! Did you finish a project at the office? Treat yourself to a bouquet of fresh flowers!

PRAYER

God, help me feel your love in such powerful, tangible ways that I have no time for comparisons. Give me confidence to parent well. Amen.

WEEK 3

Breaking Free from Generational Cycles

For God gave us a spirit not of fear but of power and love and self-control.

2 TIMOTHY 1:7 (ESV)

Did you come from a family of yellers, but you desperately want to speak gently to your children? Did your parents make poor financial choices like your grandparents? Have close family members struggled with addictions for generations? Have others hidden depression, refusing to get help? Do you know families with a history of physical or verbal abuse?

Though challenging, it's possible to break free from these unhealthy patterns.

The first step? Recognition of the problem. Whether it's a minor pattern of behavior or a devastatingly serious one, a desire to stop that cycle is the first step to breaking free.

Seek help and therapy, if needed. If you're willing to share, ask a trusted friend for prayers to end the cycle and seek an accountability partner. Strive for healthy coping skills instead of the harmful reactions you're trying to eliminate.

Most importantly? PRAY! Ask God to help you end the cycle. Celebrate little victories and persevere with power, love, and self-control. Give yourself grace when you mess up. It took years for the unhealthy habit to form; it could take time to beat it! Lean into God's strength and power to get you through when the familiar incident rears its ugly head. Depend on him. He wants to help you change. He loves you that much and more.

Eliminating unhealthy behaviors rooted in generations is tough. Don't give up! You've got this. With God's help, you can do it!

REFLECTIONS

- What unhealthy generational cycle do you want to break? List five practical steps you can take each day to eliminate that cycle completely. Treat yourself each time you accomplish one of the steps or goals to rid yourself of the unwanted behavior.
- If you feel comfortable doing so, talk with your parents or grandparents about the behavior you hope to conquer. Ask about their coping skills and childhood experiences that perpetuated the cycle. Take mental notes to help you break the cycle for your own children.
- When do you feel the most powerful? Is it when you're teaching your kids something new? Conquering a DIY project at home? Reaching new goals at work? How can that translate into power to overcome generational cycles? Perhaps tapping into your own sense of power in other situations will remind you that you are capable of establishing self-control tactics to combat the cycle you're trying to break. Write 2 Timothy 1:7 on notecards and place them around the house and at work as a reminder to stay strong and persevere.

PRAYER

Dear God, help me change unhealthy patterns in my life. Let the unwanted cycle end with ME. Amen.

Overwhelmed and Discouraged

Don't be afraid, for I am with you. Don't be discouraged,
for I am your God. I will strengthen you and help you.
I will hold you up with my victorious right hand.

ISAIAH 41:10 (NLT)

Carmelita punched in the plumber's number. "Leaking faucet," she said. The previous afternoon, she'd dialed the same number when water puddled under the dishwasher.

"I don't know how much more I can take," she thought, scooping up her teething toddler for a diaper change. Carmelita's mom lingered in the hospital with a stage four cancer diagnosis. Her husband, out of town for work, wouldn't return for four days. The middle child needed two dozen cupcakes for school the next day, the oldest one required ribbons sewn onto pointe shoes before dress rehearsal tomorrow afternoon, and taxes were due.

Do you have days like this? Moms are more overwhelmed than ever before. But nothing catches God by surprise. God knows what you're facing.

God promises to hold you up, strengthen you, and comfort you. Call out to him and tell him your needs. Your situation may not change anytime soon, but God will never leave you.

When you're overwhelmed, ask for help. Take deep breaths when the waves of discouragement wash in. Get outside for sunshine and fresh air. Stay hydrated, eat healthy, and rest.

God's got you. During those seasons of motherhood when you feel overwhelmed, cling to the promise of his presence and strength and take it one day at a time.

REFLECTIONS

- Are you in a season of discouragement? Do the challenges of motherhood or other "life situations" seem overwhelming? Though it won't change the situations, counting blessings encourages a brighter outlook and positive attitude. On one side of a piece of paper, jot down your overwhelming concerns. Across from each one, list related points of gratitude. Is your dishwasher broken? On the gratitude side, list thoughts like this: blessed to own a dishwasher, grateful to afford food that dirties dishes, thankful for mealtimes spent with family. You get the idea—try it with other overwhelming issues, too.
- If you're not in a particularly overwhelming season right now, a mom you know probably is. What can you do to help her?
- What helps you feel God's presence? Think about a specific moment recently when you felt it. How can you look for those moments each day?

PRAYER

Heavenly Father, when I'm overwhelmed and feel like I can't take any more, help me rely on your strength. Thank you for the promise of your presence. Amen.

Tuning Out Others' Opinions and Tuning In to God

> For am I now seeking the favor of people, or of God? Or am I striving to please people? If I were still trying to please people, I would not be a bond-servant of Christ.
>
> GALATIANS 1:10 (NASB)

I rarely opened the blinds in the morning, and I wouldn't let the kids outside until long after lunch. Why? I'd made the decision—about three decades ago now—to homeschool my kids. Family, close friends, and strangers challenged my decision and offered their opinions on my children's best interests. I fretted that neighbors might think of us as truant if we were outside too early in the day. I began to worry more about what others thought than where God was leading our family.

Three years into our homeschooling journey, I had a dream about my kids that solidified my school decision. I won't go into the details of the dream here, but I will say that I truly believe God used it to reveal his plans for our children's education, giving me the confidence to tune out others' opinions and heed God's plan for our lives.

Listening to worldly voices keeps us from hearing the One who deserves our attention most. When we worry more about what others think, our thoughts stray from God. Seeking to please people takes the focus away from God.

Tuning in to God takes intentionality. Reading God's Word regularly and praying daily draws us nearer to him. Focusing on Scripture and striving each day to be more like Jesus helps us feel his presence. When we're filled with his words, from his Word, we're less apt to be distracted by worldly voices.

- In what areas are you seeking to please people rather than God? What prevents you from tuning out the opinions of others and tuning in to God's plan? How can you make it a priority to seek the Lord's voice instead of those that would distract you from his plan for your life?
- What holds you back from having consistent Bible reading time and a fervent prayer life? How can you make changes to incorporate these two activities into your daily routine? In what ways can you go deeper into God's Word, and how can you purposefully put into practice what you read?
- Think back to a time when God revealed a plan for your family that was contrary to the voices surrounding you. What helped you tune out worldly voices? What helped you stand firm in your decision or choice? How did you see God work in your family as a result of that decision?

PRAYER

Dear God, help me seek your favor instead of the
favor of those around me. Help me tune out opinions
that contradict your plan for my family. Amen.

Body Image—Struggling to Feel Comfortable in Our Own Skin

The Lord doesn't see things the way you see them. People judge by outward appearance, but the Lord looks at the heart.

1 SAMUEL 16:7 (NLT)

"We're taking family portraits tomorrow," June said, "and I don't have anything to wear. I haven't lost this baby weight and nothing looks good on me."

June's comment brought forth declarations from other moms gathered for playgroup.

"I hate pictures of myself," said one. "I've tried whiteners, but my teeth are so dingy."

"At least your teeth are straight," said another. "My parents couldn't afford braces, and my teeth are so crooked."

"Pictures show all my acne scars," said yet another of the mothers.

"You cover the few scars with makeup well," encouraged one mom. Then she added, "No amount of paint can hide my freckles, and nothing tames this frizzy hair."

Sound familiar? Moms have struggled with body image for centuries. Cultural norms elevate our appearances over what's truly important. Yet God reveals what's important in 1 Samuel 16:7—the heart.

God wants our hearts fully committed to him. When we've accepted Jesus Christ, God's only Son, into our lives, the Holy Spirit dwells within us, revealing the fruit of the Spirit: love, joy, peace, patience, kindness, goodness, faithfulness, gentleness, and self-control. Outside appearances don't matter to God. Our attitudes and thoughts and kindness and love toward others do.

Moms will probably always struggle to a degree with body image issues, but we can be much happier when we look at ourselves and others the way God does, bypassing outward appearances and going straight for the heart!

REFLECTIONS

- What body image issues do you struggle with the most? Why do you think those trouble you? What are you grateful for today?
- What would help you see yourself as God sees you? If God complimented you on your heart, what would he say? In what ways can you use those words to change how you feel about yourself?
- How can you redirect your focus when negative body image thoughts enter your mind? Try this: first, memorize the fruit of the Spirit verses, Galatians 5:22-23. Then, when a thought like, "Gosh, I hate my frizzy hair" pops into your head, say instead: "I love others. I exude joy. I am a peacemaker. I am patient. I am kind. I am good. I am faithful. I am gentle. I practice self-control." (And if some of those statements don't ring true, consider working on them instead of dwelling on body image!)

PRAYER

God, it's hard not to fret over my appearance. Help me see myself the way you do. Thank you for loving me inside and out! Amen.

Don't Worry, Don't Fret—Trust God

The Lord is my strength and my shield; my heart trusts
in him, and I am helped. Therefore my heart celebrates,
and I give thanks to him with my song.

PSALM 28:7 (CSB)

"This snowstorm's bad," my oldest son said. "It's dark, and the only way
to navigate is by the taillights of the 18-wheeler in front of me. I'll stop
when I find a—"

Click. The call ended, and my heart skipped a beat. Did Jeremy
crash into the truck ahead of him? Did he careen over a cliff or slam
against a tree?

It's hard not to worry as a mom, right? I'll fret over something simple, like whether dinner will be ready on time so we can get to church.
And I can full-blown worry over my kids' safety, health, choices, academic success, potential spouses, and so much more.

But worrying solves nothing. Fretting doesn't fix anything. And
Jesus commands us not to. We may feel like we're barely holding on,
but God's holding on to us. He supports us, sustains us, protects us, and
comforts us. We are helped because he is our strength. Our situation
may or may not change, but when we put our trust in the ever-loving
arms of our Father, we can know with certainty that he will work all
things together for good, according to his purpose. He cares for our

needs and supplies them. He will never leave us. We can trust that he is always good. And that's worth celebrating!

REFLECTIONS

- Is there something that you are worried about at this very moment? Can your anxious thoughts solve or eliminate the problem? Obviously, that's a rhetorical question, because worrying doesn't solve problems. After talking to God about your worries, can you think of actual steps to take that might help the situation? What can help you trust God with the outcome?
- Think back to other worries you've experienced since you became a mom. How did God see you through each one of those situations? In what ways was he your strength and shield? How did he help you then? And how can you transfer that knowledge to your worries of today?
- Do you believe that God loves your children infinitely more than you ever could? I hope you answered with a resounding "yes." With that knowledge, how can your heart celebrate and give thanks to God?

PRAYER

God, teach me to trust you. Take away my anxious thoughts and help me focus on you instead. You are good and worthy of my trust. Amen.

Insecurities Be Gone—We Are Valued by God

I praise you because I am fearfully and wonderfully made.
PSALM 139:14 (NIV)

Lynn watched her five-year-old approach the other kids on the playground and overheard a child say, "You can't play with us," just before running to the swings. Her entourage joined her. The incident brought back painful memories, as Lynn recalled hearing the same words directed at her in fourth grade and then in seventh, overhearing the popular girls discussing her ugly shoes. A financially struggling rancher's daughter, Lynn never seemed to fit in.

Her insecurities followed her into adulthood, where she often felt less educated, less beautiful, less popular, less interesting, or just *less* . . .

Whispered insecurities are lies from the enemy. The enemy wants us to feel less than, but in God's Kingdom that's impossible! God made each one of us, fearfully and wonderfully. He values and loves us like a treasure.

God loves us so much that he sent his Son to earth to take on the sins of the world. Jesus died on the cross for our sins, paying our debt, so that by accepting him as Lord and Savior, we can have eternal life in heaven. We're that precious to God! He calls us his own children and adopts us into his family.

Tear down the wall of insecurity surrounding your heart, brick by brick, lie by lie, and praise God for making you. You are wonderful in his eyes, and he loves you just the way you are. You are valued by the Most High God.

REFLECTIONS

- What insecurities do you struggle with? Can you pinpoint specific incidents that caused you to develop those insecurities? How can you forgive the person or persons who hurt you and put the incident behind you for good?
- In what situations do you feel most insecure? What can you do before you enter those circumstances to guard your mind and heart from insecurities creeping in? For example, memorize this week's verse. And the very moment an insecure thought materializes, first, stomp that lie into the ground, then repeat the verse over and over in your mind.
- What's your favorite way to praise the Lord? Through music played loudly in the car? In quiet prayer time on the front porch? With written or spoken words to God? How can you find new ways to praise him and express your gratitude for making you fearfully and wonderfully?

PRAYER

God, I praise you because I am fearfully and wonderfully made—by YOU, the Most High God. Help me believe that promise and not the lies of the enemy. Amen.

Get Rid of Unhealthy Practices—
Honor God with Your Body

Do you not know that your bodies are temples of the Holy Spirit, who is in you, whom you have received from God? You are not your own; you were bought at a price. Therefore honor God with your bodies.

1 CORINTHIANS 6:19–20 (NIV)

My brother started drinking alcohol in high school. Continuing into college and adulthood, Timothy hid his alcoholism for years, until his liver began showing signs of early cirrhosis. "If you don't stop drinking, you'll die," his doctor said bluntly.

Kind and compassionate, brilliant, and possessing a servant's heart, Timothy struggled to stop. He lost the battle at the age of 47. For my own reasons, I'd chosen not to partake of alcoholic beverages. I couldn't completely grasp my brother's addictive nature.

Until I tried to give up diet soda, that is. When a mild case of Covid-19 took away my senses of taste and smell, I decided it was the ideal time to kick the habit of drinking more than a dozen cans a day. Covid made the initial halt easy. But for months and even years afterward, I continued to crave soda. I'd had no idea I had my own addictions.

Do you have unhealthy practices that you need to deal with? Yours might not be life-threatening like my brother's or as damaging to the body as mine, but do you struggle with harmful practices? An eating disorder? Smoking? Vaping? Consuming too many sweets or excessive junk food? Pornography? Immoral behavior? Infidelity? Not getting enough exercise?

Seek help if you need it. Remind yourself that as a mother, your children are always watching and learning from your behavior. Call on God's strength to fight the battle. And don't give up!

REFLECTIONS

- What unhealthy practices plague you? How do these practices affect your role as a mom? How are they damaging to your children? Who do you know who can keep you accountable for making healthy lifestyle changes?
- What's the first step that you need to take to stop your unhealthy practice? For example, if you lead a sedentary lifestyle, how can you begin to get more active each day? If you consume too many sweets, how can you remove that temptation from your life? Do you need to adjust your social calendar to limit your exposure to alcohol and tobacco?
- What does it mean to you to honor God with your body? What things do you need to stop and what things do you need to start to heed God's command to see your body as a sacred temple? What verse can you memorize to help you remember that God loves you and wants you to take care of yourself?

PRAYER

God, help me treat my body like the temple you deserve.
Show me areas where I need to make changes so
that I can honor you with my body. Amen.

Dealing with Isolation and Loneliness

She gave this name to the LORD who spoke to her:
"You are the God who sees me," for she said,
"I have now seen the One who sees me."

GENESIS 16:13 (NIV)

Have you experienced lonely moments since you became a mom? I have, which is odd because in those first few years especially, it feels like we're never ever alone! Something about being responsible for little human beings, and being removed from most adults if you're a stay-at-home mom, often leads to feelings of isolation and loneliness.

On the other end of the mom spectrum, with busy teenagers driving on their own or young adults leaving the nest for college or careers, isolation and loneliness seep in, too.

Whether your house is devoid of other humans or half a dozen children clamor at your feet, there's one thing we can all count on: we're never alone because God is with us. God sees us, God loves us, and God will never leave us.

In Genesis, pregnant Egyptian maidservant Hagar flees to the desert alone. The angel of the Lord meets her, comforts her, and encourages her to return to Abram and Sarai. Hagar responds with the words of this week's verse.

My sweet friend, we are never alone. Our God keeps his eyes on us and watches over us night and day. We may feel lonely for a time, but we are never alone. God is there. Lean into him and feel his presence. Let him wrap his arms around you and comfort you. He sees you.

REFLECTIONS

- What makes you feel alone or unseen? In opposition, what actions and words make you feel validated and seen?
- How can you redirect your thoughts to help you feel God's presence every day? God wants you to know he sees you and loves you. Will you look for him today?
- If you're an isolated mom with a newborn, or a mom with teens who are never home, or a mom with an empty nest, what steps can you take to alleviate the pangs of loneliness? Have you tried meeting face-to-face with other moms in similar situations, making phone calls and reaching out on social media while the baby sleeps, or finding a volunteer outlet where you can meet like-minded moms? Do you practice self-care? Fresh air daily, staying hydrated, eating healthy, and getting rest help energize the body and give you strength to get through a challenging season.

PRAYER

God, thank you for seeing me. When I feel lonely, help me know you are there. Give me strength to get through the lonely seasons. Amen.

You Are a Masterpiece, on Purpose for a Purpose

For we are God's masterpiece. He has created us anew in Christ Jesus, so we can do the good things he planned for us long ago.
EPHESIANS 2:10 (NLT)

"I never thought I'd have a master's degree in journalism and end up spending my time picking someone else's nose." Kelly chuckled, wrangling her two-year-old's face into the tissue.

Deb wiped peanut butter off her son's cheek, the picnic table, her cell phone, and her shorts. "I hear ya, friend."

At some point during motherhood, you've probably wrestled with the question, "What is my purpose?" God created us to glorify him. *That* is our purpose. We are his masterpiece. He is crazy about us, and he had plans for us long before our birth! He created us to bring glory to him, and he has a purpose for each one of us. In whatever stage of motherhood we're in, we live out our purpose by worshipping him with our whole heart, living a life that is pleasing to him, serving him, and telling others the good news of his Son, Jesus Christ.

In some mom seasons, it's all we can do to wipe a nose or cheek, talk to our child about Jesus, and kiss that same little face goodnight. In other seasons, we might cure cancer, safely deliver 50 children home on a school bus, design a luxury resort, or witness to hundreds in a foreign country.

God has big plans for us, and raising little ones may be the biggest part of his plan. Live each day as God's chosen masterpiece and glorify the One who made you.

- How often do you question your purpose in life? Aside from glorifying God, do you feel your purpose has changed over the years? Were you happy with those changes or unhappy? What helps you feel like you are living out your God-given purpose?
- In some Christian communities, people like to say, "We're made on purpose, with a purpose, for a purpose." How can you relate that to your current season of motherhood? Is it harder for you to see God's purpose in your life than it is to see it in members of your family or circle of friends? If you answered yes, why do you think that's so?
- Are there times when you feel more like a mess than a masterpiece? God knew the different seasons of your life before you were born. Remind yourself that he's crazy about you, his masterpiece, by memorizing this week's verse.

Dear Maker of masterpieces, thank you for creating me to do good things. Help me live out the purpose for which you created me. Amen.

WEEK 12

Saddle Up and Be Brave

Be strong and courageous. Do not be afraid; do not be discouraged,
for the Lord your God will be with you wherever you go.
JOSHUA 1:9 (NIV)

Several months after we welcomed our fourth child, I devised a plan to ensure that I was giving the older kids individual attention. David and I took turns participating in "special time" with the other three. For one of her activities, Jenifer chose horseback riding, which sounds like a fun bonding time—except that I'm afraid of horses.

Actually, I'm not afraid of the horse, just the riding part! I prayed beforehand and during, and it's a memory we still treasure. It took a lot of bravery and leaning into God to get me through the ride, but I'm glad I did it.

Whatever you're facing—horseback riding, surgery, a move across the country, speaking in front of a big group of people, an impending divorce, an unwanted diagnosis for you or a family member—you can be confident that God will be with you. God is bigger than whatever you're facing. You can be confident that God is in control. No matter what happens, no matter what the outcome is, no matter how difficult the challenge—God is right by your side the entire time.

We can trust God when he tells us to be strong and courageous, because it's *his* strength we're leaning into. We don't have to be strong on our own. We just have to trust him. So, saddle up and be brave! God's got your back!

- What kind of scary challenge are you facing right now? How often do you talk to God about the situation? What other verses can you memorize besides the one for this week that can help calm your fears? (A quick, online search for "Bible verses about being brave" will bring up a host of helpful Scripture to commit to memory! Like Psalm 56:3 (NIV): "When I am afraid, I put my trust in you.")
- Think back to a recent time when you were afraid. How did God prove faithful to his promise to be with you during that circumstance? How can that memory help you get through fearful times in the future?
- Who are some people you know who've faced challenges or circumstances that required an extra portion of bravery? How did you see God working in their lives during that time?

PRAYER

God, remind me of your presence when I feel afraid. Help me be brave when I face challenges or new situations. Thank you for being with me always. Amen.

The Blues

The Lord your God is in your midst, a mighty one who will
save; he will rejoice over you with gladness; he will quiet
you by his love; he will exult over you with loud singing.

ZEPHANIAH 3:17 (ESV)

Virginia sat on the front porch, tears spilling onto her lap. Her mom, an Alzheimer's patient for the last five years, had recently been transferred to a hospice facility. Virginia tried to gather her thoughts before driving over to feed her mom breakfast.

The Bible says we'll experience troubles in this world, and many of those difficulties bring great heartache. My friend, God catches each one of our tears. We can take our sadness to him, because he cares deeply for us. God is right there, holding us close. He comforts us in whatever trial or difficulty we're facing. Our situation may or may not change, but he promises to quiet us with his love. He loves us so much that he sings over each one of us!

(If you're struggling with depression, situational or clinical, I urge you to seek medical help. You have options to consider, and a medical professional will know how to advise you. If you feel that your "baby blues" might possibly be a more severe case of postpartum depression, please seek help from your doctor. For your sake, and for the sake of your family, seeking help is the right thing to do.)

God is big enough to handle our sadness and our problems. Hold on to his love.

- What's going on right now that causes you sadness? How does it comfort you to know that God is in the midst of your sadness? What helps you feel his presence? Close your eyes and imagine God singing over you. What are the words of his song?
- What cheers you up when you're feeling blue? What can you do to change your perspective today that will offer consolation for your sadness? Counting our blessings often helps take our mind off of our sadness. Make a point to be grateful today.
- If you're not in a season of sadness currently, you probably know a mom who is experiencing difficult times. What can you do to remind her of God's love? How can you use a previous time of sadness in your life to help you empathize with her?

PRAYER

Dear God, when the waves of sadness come and tears spill over, quiet my sobs with your love so that I can hear you singing over me. Thank you for never leaving me. Amen.

Overcoming Disappointment

And we know that God causes everything to work
together for the good of those who love God and
are called according to his purpose for them.

ROMANS 8:28 (NLT)

"I didn't get the job," Mickay told her husband. "I thought my qualifications and experience were perfect for this one. I just don't understand."

Disappointments sting. Especially when we've prayed about an issue and believe it's in line with God's plan. Sometimes, God's plan doesn't match up with our plans. But we can trust that God's plans are best. Even when it doesn't feel that way, even when we're really disappointed, even when things don't seem to be going our way. God's plans are always best.

God is a good father. He delights in giving us good gifts. He knows the desires of our hearts. He doesn't just want *good* for us; he wants THE BEST. God's ways are not always our ways, but we can trust that they are best for us.

Disappointment sometimes happens when we put our hope in people or circumstances. When we put our hope in God and trust in his goodness and faithfulness, we can push back the darkness of disappointment and walk in the light of the Lord.

God promises to work all circumstances together for our good. That doesn't mean each circumstance will *be* good. Some will cause huge disappointment. Remembering this week's verse and talking to God can help us accept disappointment in time and trust him despite the circumstance.

REFLECTIONS

- What recent situation brought you disappointment? How did you respond? Did you talk to a trusted mentor or someone you respect about your disappointment? Did you talk to God about your disappointment? Talking with others—especially God—can help alleviate the feeling of disappointment. Friends or family members who've been through similar situations can often offer a different perspective to help you through a time of sadness.
- Think back to a time when God worked good out of a bad situation. Was it hard to see God's hand in the matter early on? How can you use past moments of faithfulness from God to remind you that he is trustworthy and good?
- How difficult is it for you to accept when things don't work out as you'd planned? What helps you remember that God's plans are always best, even when it doesn't feel that way?

PRAYER

God, remind me that you are working all things for my good,
especially when circumstances seem to scream otherwise.
Give me strength to face disappointments. Amen.

Letting Go of Past Mistakes and Regrets

This means that anyone who belongs to Christ has become a new person. The old life is gone; a new life has begun!

2 CORINTHIANS 5:17 (NLT)

"I wish I hadn't said those words."

"I regret doing that."

"I should've responded differently."

If you're like me, you've had conversations, either in your head or with others, that used words similar to those above. We all have things in our past that we regret. It's hard not to make mistakes, and some of our missteps are bigger than others.

The Bible is rife with people who made mistakes. Paul regretted his persecution of believers before he came to know Christ. Sarai wished she hadn't laughed in disbelief when God said she would have a baby. Peter grieved over his denial of Christ.

Unwise decisions prompt regret. Past sins cause regret. Regret can paralyze us with disappointment in ourselves and hinder us from moving forward. But the Bible assures us that when we admit that we are a sinner and accept Christ as our Savior, we are a new person. Our sins are forgiven. We can move past our regrets.

Instead of dwelling on our past mistakes, God wants us to look ahead at what great things are to come. Paul, the former persecutor of new Christians, said, in Philippians 3:13 (NIV), "But one thing I do: Forgetting what is behind and straining toward what is ahead." God has good things planned ahead for us. Let's leave regrets in the past where they belong.

REFLECTIONS

- What regrets from the past plague you? Have you asked God to forgive you for those sins and mistakes? If you've done so, let Psalm 103:12 (NIV) be a reminder that God has removed your sins "as far as the east is from the west."
- What steps have you taken to let go of past mistakes and regrets? If you've already asked God for forgiveness, consider whether there is someone who was affected by your mistake that you should also seek forgiveness from. Write down your regrets, pray, shred the document, and move forward!
- If your regret involves something you wish you would have done, how can you work toward making that happen in your life now? If your regret involves current behavior you wish you could change, what can you do today to take a step toward making that happen? Is there something you need to say to someone to undo a past mistake?

PRAYER

God, please forgive my past sins. Help me feel forgiven and loved and treasured, despite my many mistakes. Help me let go of regret and see that I am a new person in you. Amen.

Moving Past Mom Guilt

If we confess our sins, he is faithful and just to forgive us
our sins and to cleanse us from all unrighteousness.

1 JOHN 1:9 (ESV)

Five-year-old Jeb Daniel snuck into the den past bedtime and announced, "I can't sleep." I turned off my computer and climbed into the double rocking chair with him to snuggle a bit. Anxious to get back to work, I silently groaned with each fidget. Finally, I snapped. "Jeb Daniel, you're never going to fall asleep if you won't be still."

"I'm just so itchy, Mommy."

I pulled up his pajama shirt. Hives! All over his back. I'm not sure why he didn't tell me about his itchiness initially, but I felt like a horrible mom for losing my temper.

Mommy guilt is miserable. When we hurt the ones we love most, our shortcomings crush us. Sometimes, we set unrealistic expectations for ourselves as moms, allowing us to fall prey to guilt's unwanted meanness. Other times, our sins and mistakes grieve and burden us.

God doesn't want us to dwell on past mistakes and guilt. When we admit our failures to God, confessing our sins, God wipes the slate clean. He remembers our sin no more. Unfortunately, though, *we* often hang on to guilt.

God's mercy is new every morning. Once forgiven, we can move forward, leaving the past behind us. God wants us to walk in his light each day. Dragging guilt with us casts darkness into our hearts. Let go of guilt and latch onto his forgiveness instead.

- What guilt are you carrying? Have you shared your concerns with God and asked forgiveness? Have you asked forgiveness from those you've wronged? Why do you think you're holding on to guilt? When God says we are cleansed from *all* unrighteousness, why is it so difficult to accept the word *all*?
- Is there someone you have wronged recently? What can you do this week to fix that? Is it hard for you to say the words, "I'm sorry"? If you didn't grow up in a family that apologized readily, you may find that challenging. Practice apologizing for little mistakes and apologies for bigger ones will get easier.
- Why do you think mommy guilt is often more challenging than other guilt we encounter? If Jesus talked to you about mommy guilt, what do you think he would say? How can you keep those words in mind for the next time you face guilt?

PRAYER

God, when I confess my sins, help me feel forgiven. Thank you for Jesus, who paid the price for my sins. Amen.

MOVING PAST MOM GUILT   43

When It's Out of Your Control

"For my thoughts are not your thoughts, neither are your
ways my ways," declares the LORD. "As the heavens
are higher than the earth, so are my ways higher than
your ways and my thoughts than your thoughts."

ISAIAH 55:8–9 (NIV)

"We're moving to Hawaii." David waved a copy of his orders. Thrilled about getting our first choice for my husband's next duty station with the Navy, we started making plans. Kayak transportation for David—check. Base housing lined up—check. Church and homeschool co-op located—check.

And then—David's orders got changed. "Poulsbo, Washington," David announced.

Some things are out of our control. Plans change. The unexpected happens. An unwanted diagnosis comes in. A sick baby halts work plans. A teenager goes astray. Luggage gets lost.

God's sovereignty, his authority and rule over all of creation, means he can and will work everything together for our good. Despite what happens to us that's out of our control, we can trust that God knows every detail, and his plans are best. When we let go of control and trust that God in his infinite power will see us through the situation, we can rest with confidence that he's got this! We don't have to work it out on our own. God's ways are always so much better than ours, because he is a good Father and loves us immeasurably.

A situation you can't control might result in tears, anger, anxiety, and more. God's big enough to handle all of that, too. Let him.

REFLECTIONS

- Is there something happening in your life right now that is out of your control? Do you have a hard time accepting that? What is your typical reaction when the unexpected happens that you can't control? Do you feel like you can respond more favorably if you recognize and accept that God's ways are higher than yours?
- Do you have a more difficult time relinquishing control when it relates to kids, work, spouse, or outside-the-home activities? How can you learn to let go of control in small increments, working up to giving God total control of your family?
- When did you see a specific example of God's higher ways in a family situation? How long did it take you to recognize that his ways were higher than your original way of thinking? Were you able to admit that recognition to God? Going forward, what can help you trust God more?

PRAYER

God, please give me the strength to get through situations that are out of my control. Help me trust you with my cares. Amen.

Relationship Building

" 'And you shall love the Lord your God with all your heart
and with all your soul and with all your mind and with all your
strength.' The second is this: 'You shall love your neighbor as
yourself.' There is no other commandment greater than these."

MARK 12:30–31 (ESV)

Marlitta opened the door. Her across-the-street neighbor and best friend Ana asked, "Can I snitch a block of butter from you? I'm baking—" She paused, looking at Marlitta. "You look awful. You okay?"

"Yeah, I've got a bigger emergency. I think I have another kidney stone."

"I've got the kids," Ana said. "You get to a doctor."

Having friends when an emergency arises, like single-parent Marlitta with no family nearby, is invaluable to moms. As busy as we get, finding time for relationships outside of family can be challenging, but forming camaraderie with like-minded women gives us the chance to interact with other adults who have similar interests and passions. It's also an opportunity to give and receive encouragement, support, answers to questions, and fun fellowship. Relationship building takes time when you're a busy mom, but the rewards outweigh the challenges.

Jesus said the second greatest commandment is to love others. Loving people well honors God with our obedience. Loving others like Jesus does teaches our kids to emulate him, too. To have good friends we need to *be* good friends. Moms need friends for encouragement in the difficult times and strength in the challenging ones. And treating our neighbors like ourselves just makes the world a better place.

- How have your relationships with others (besides family) changed since becoming a mom? Do you find it more difficult to build and grow relationships as a mom? What is the most challenging aspect? What can you change that would make you a better friend?
- Recall some of your most fun experiences with friends since becoming a mom. Did it take effort and maneuvering to work out all the details? Did the blessing of the experience outweigh the challenge? Do you initiate most of your friend-time or do your friends? Would you like to change that? How have your friendships given you strength as a mom?
- What do you think Jesus meant by loving your neighbor like yourself? In what specific ways do you put that directive into practice with your friends and others you come in contact with? How can you love others better?

PRAYER

Jesus, thank you for calling me "friend." Teach me how to be a better friend to those around me. Teach me to love like you. Amen.

When Relationships Fall Apart

Wait for the LORD; be strong and take heart and wait for the LORD.
PSALM 27:14 (NIV)

Paige enjoyed her friendship with Miriam. Both empty nesters, the women spent time together over coffee after work and chatted on the phone often. One day, Paige confided the devastating effects of her husband's recent emotional affair. Later, when someone questioned the husband's attentiveness to another woman, Paige mistakenly thought Miriam instigated rumors. Embarrassed by it all, she ended her friendship with Miriam. The only good news: Paige and her husband reconciled after months of separation.

Have you lost an important relationship? A best friend, a spouse, a treasured family member? Losing a valued relationship, especially one that you thought would last a lifetime, can be devastating. God sees and he cares. He loves you with a never-ending love. Let him wrap you in his arms. Take comfort in your heavenly Father's abiding love. Human relationships may end, but God's love for you never will. That's a promise you can believe.

Conversely, if you've felt the need to end a relationship, take heart in knowing that God will see you through that situation. Knowing when to end a friendship is vital to a mom's mental health. Toxic friends who drain your energy strain your ability to properly care for the family.

Extra-needy friends take much time away from family. Unkind friends just aren't fun to be around!

If you're hurting from a lost relationship, my friend, wait for the Lord. He will never let you go.

REFLECTIONS

- Have you ever been or are you currently in a broken relationship? Severed relationships hurt and require some sort of attention. What comforts you? How have you turned to the Lord with your brokenness? What helpful Scriptures have you read? Have you talked to a trusted friend, church staff member, or counselor?
- How does this week's verse give you strength to face a broken relationship? How can you wait patiently on the Lord? What can you do in real time to help yourself begin to heal from the loss? What helps you feel God's presence during your pain? How do you know with assurance that God's love is never-ending, everlasting, all-encompassing?
- The breakdown of a relationship can leave the hurt person feeling at fault or lonely or unworthy. What helps you negate these feelings? What can you do to feel valued and loved by God, your kids, and other family and friends?

PRAYER

God, this hurts. My heart is broken. I need you. Help me wait on you. Thank you for your love that never ends. Amen.

When Interruptions Disrupt

"For I know the plans I have for you," declares the LORD, "plans to prosper you and not to harm you, plans to give you hope and a future."

JEREMIAH 29:11 (NIV)

"Two more minutes, Jeremy, then it's time for science." When the newborn demanded nursing and three-year-old Jenifer required a clothing change, Jeremy escaped to check on his pet lizard. I'd planned a fun unit on insects, mostly because my husband, the entomologist, could help with the homeschool lessons.

Seconds later, Jeremy shrieked and yelled, "A hundred ants are attacking my lizard!"

"Not now, Jeremy, it's time for us to talk about insects." I realized the absurdity of my response, placed the baby in the bassinet, and led Jenifer to the carport for a hands-on lesson on insects and reptiles.

Interruptions fluster even the most seasoned moms. One more interruption often feels like the tipping point when we've had an overwhelming day. What if these little interruptions, and sometimes catastrophic ones, are part of God's plan? What if we could see them as lessons to learn for ourselves, teaching moments for our kids, or opportunities to draw closer to God?

God's plans for us are always good. God has our best interests in mind, despite the annoying interruptions. This week's Bible verse isn't saying that life won't be hard and everything will be rosy, but it does mean that we can count on God's plans to be best. And we can count on God to be with us through every interruption.

- How well do you handle interruptions? What is your initial response to an interruption? In what ways could you handle interruptions better? How do interruptions affect you personally? How do they affect your family? How does your faith help you deal with interruptions?
- Think for a moment about the woman in the Bible who came to a well to get water. When a man interrupted her daily chore, her life changed forever. (You can read about that in John 4:1-42.) Can you think of a minor interruption that impacted you greatly? Have you experienced a major interruption that changed the course of your life?
- How can you see God directing your life's path? Do you recognize his hand in the little things as well as the big things? How does it comfort you to know that God has good plans for you? What helps you believe the promise of Jeremiah 29:11 when interruptions come your way?

PRAYER

God, help me look for and recognize your presence in life's interruptions. Give me strength, patience, and wisdom to look for the lessons they have to teach. Thank you that your plans are good. Amen.

When Parenting Styles Differ

Don't copy the behavior and customs of this world, but let God
transform you into a new person by changing the way you think.
ROMANS 12:2 (NLT)

Penny ordered fast food for her kids and sat near the indoor playground. When an adult cartoon show on a nearby television blared into the dining room with expletives and inappropriate language, Penny politely asked the manager to turn it off.

The manager scowled but complied, mumbling to the teenage employees as he walked away.

Have you ever been met with opposition about your parenting style? Or teased because of a parenting choice? God gave us the responsibility of raising our children. We can and should raise our children in the saving knowledge of Jesus Christ as Lord and Savior. That just might mean different parenting styles than those of the world around us. Romans 12:2 warns us not to chase after the pleasures and possessions of this world. We can't live like the rest of the world and follow Jesus.

When we heed this week's verse, we change our thinking and therefore actions to reflect a life that follows Jesus. That shapes our parenting styles.

But even parenting styles among believers differ. As believers who love people like Jesus does, we can continue to love our brothers and sisters in Christ who parent differently than we do, without conflict and opposition. And we can love those of the world, just like God does, without conforming to their lifestyles.

Trust God's voice about your parenting style. His thoughts are the only ones that matter.

REFLECTIONS

- How does your parenting style differ from that of your close friends with children? How does it differ from worldly standards? How does your faith guide your parenting choices and style? What gives you confidence and strength to stand up to others when your parenting style is challenged?
- Have you ever been dismissed by other parents or friends because of a parenting choice? How did you respond? How do you respond to those you meet who have different parenting styles and standards? Is there anything about your parenting style you want to change? New ideas you want to initiate?
- How can you change your thinking to avoid seeking the pleasures and possessions of the world? What lifestyle changes has your family made to avoid living like the world does? How would you describe the new life God gave you when you accepted Jesus as Savior? What transformations took place inwardly and outwardly?

PRAYER

God, help me honor and glorify you with my parenting
style. Turn my heart away from the snares of the world
and keep my mind focused on you. Amen.

The Gift of Being Present in the Moment

Be very careful, then, how you live—not as unwise but as wise, making the most of every opportunity, because the days are evil.
EPHESIANS 5:15–16 (NIV)

After a long day at the amusement park, Jeremy and Jenifer got a second wind back at the hotel. Jumping from bed to bed, they giggled with glee. David and I stood close to ward off injury. We added pillows to the floor between the beds and told the kids to watch out for alligators in the moat.

Several days later while driving home, I asked the kids to name their favorite part of the vacation. "Jumping on the beds in the hotel."

David looked at me and smiled. "We could've saved a lot of money and just hung out in the hotel room."

I winked back at my hubby and said, "I'm glad we got involved in their game."

I don't always get it right as a parent. In fact, I've made many mistakes. But I try hard to be present in the moment with my kids as often as possible. Dishes can wait until later, but the mud puddle to splash in won't last. Avoid sweeping a little longer and climb in the blanket fort with the kids. Put away the laptop and cell phone and stay up past bedtime to watch a movie with the middle schooler. Skip your favorite drama series and grab late-night milkshakes with the teenager in pajamas.

Recognize each moment with your child as a gift from God and actively engage to make treasured memories.

REFLECTIONS

- How difficult is it for you to stop what you're doing to engage with your kids? How do you respond when your little one asks you to play or your bigger ones want to go for coffee or a treat?
- What aspects of your children elicit a sense of wonder? What parts of God's beautiful creation inspire a sense of wonder in your mind and heart? How can you "be still" more often to capture the moments of wonder with your children? How can you pay attention more to your children's interests in order to engage with them in those areas?
- Practically speaking, how can you make the most of every opportunity with your children and still attend to other responsibilities? How can you manage your time and priorities better to make more time to be present with the kids?

PRAYER

Dear God, with so many responsibilities, sometimes it's hard to be in the moment with my kids. Remind me that the time with my children is brief. Help me seize opportunities for memories. Amen.

Juggling Career and Motherhood

Show me the right path, O LORD; point out the road for me to follow. Lead me by your truth and teach me, for you are the God who saves me. All day long I put my hope in you.

PSALM 25:4-5 (NLT)

When Kelsey's sitter moved away, she struggled to find childcare for her elementary-aged children. She begged God to show her the right person to care for her kids. Soon, a new shift opened at Kelsey's workplace, allowing her to start and finish work earlier, just in time to pick up the kids from school.

Juggling career and motherhood is hard. Very hard. There's no other way to put it. It's. Just. Hard.

God sees and knows your challenges. He's with you in the trenches. He hears you and answers when you call to him. Lean into God. Put your hope in him every minute of every day. The struggles are real, but God is bigger.

A few tips: Compartmentalize—focus on work while there and be present in the moment with the kids otherwise. Stay as organized as possible. Ask for help from others. Remember self-care. And give yourself grace!

You may feel like your career and motherhood move in slow motion or at race car speed, but God will never ever let you go. Hang on tight to him, pray diligently, read his Word. He promises to be with you always. When you remain in him, he won't let you down. He'll guide you on each step of your journey, whether creeping along or speeding by.

REFLECTIONS

- What's the most difficult part of juggling motherhood and your career? How do you balance both? What parts of the juggling act have you mastered? Where do you still need work? Do you struggle to leave work at the office? How do you practice being present in the moment with the kids when you put on your mommy hat?
- How willing are you to ask others for help? What self-care practices do you fit in that help you juggle motherhood and your career? What organizational tips help you the most? What others do you need to implement to better balance career and motherhood?
- How has God helped you balance job responsibilities and mother-hood demands? What steps can you take to depend on him during these challenging seasons of motherhood? In what ways do you interact with the Lord before making an important career or mommy decision?

PRAYER

Dear Father, please help me manage motherhood and my career such that you are always first. Lead me each step of the way. I put my hope in you. Amen.

No Time for Self-Care

In my distress I called upon the LORD; to my God I cried for help. From his temple he heard my voice, and my cry to him reached his ears.

PSALM 18:6 (ESV)

Stay-at-home mom Haley and her husband Tom adopted two siblings, Elana and Manuel. The parents knew prior to adoption that Manuel's special needs required extra attention. "Tom, I love our family, but I barely have time to catch my breath." Haley sighed. "I can't even shave both legs on the same day, and I can't remember the last time I washed my hair."

Can you relate to Haley's distress? Becoming a mom adds immeasurable blessings but often subtracts any free time for personal care. The responsibility of caring for other humans can be overwhelming and time-consuming. As a mom, when something has to go, we usually skip self-care time. Time is a precious commodity, and we hesitate to use it on ourselves. It's a conundrum.

One with no perfect answer.

God can handle conundrums. He hears our distressed cry for help when we're drowning in responsibilities. Call out to him first and foremost, and then try these tips. Some take longer than others, but even a few minutes a day of self-care can invigorate, refresh, and change your whole outlook. Go for a quick walk or run. Dance in your room. Exercise.

Garden. Work on puzzles. Watch a movie. Get a facial. Try a new recipe. Make a list of blessings.

Cry out to God. He hears you.

REFLECTIONS

- How can you have assurance that God hears your prayers? What specific answers to prayers have you received in the past? What helps you hear God's voice? Is it during the quietness of prayer time? Reading God's Word? Praising him with music or dance? Getting outside into the wonder of nature? What steps can you take to better hear from God? How can you draw closer to him?

- What relieves your stress as a mom? What's your favorite method of self-care? How can you find ways to practice self-care activities without feeling guilty? Have you thought about swapping out childcare with a good friend for the purpose of freeing up some much-needed self-care time?

- Do you wait until you're distressed to call out to the Lord? Are you more faithful with prayer during "good" times or "bad" times? How can you make a regular habit of communicating with God?

PRAYER

God, help me take care of myself, especially when I get overwhelmed. Thank you for being a God who hears. Thank you for comforting me in my distress. Amen.

When Children Turn from Their Faith

"Restrain your voice from weeping and your eyes from
tears, for your work will be rewarded," declares the LORD.
"They will return from the land of the enemy."

JEREMIAH 31:16 (NIV)

"I worry when Anita travels," Mia said. "Ever since she told me she no longer believes in God, I get so anxious for her safety and eternity."

Gayle touched her friend's shoulder with compassion. "I know you want her to come back to the Lord, Mia. I pray for her all the time."

Even if you don't have adult children who have walked away from their faith, chances are great that you know someone who does.

What can you do? Keep loving on 'em and pray fervently against the enemy. Fight back with nonstop prayers for your child to accept the truth of God's Word and to walk back into God's light. Your heart hurts and your eyes leak tears of sadness. Know that God sees you and God sees your prodigal child.

Nothing can separate us from the love of God. God loves you, and God loves your wayward child. Passionately, with an everlasting love. No matter their mistakes or sins or resistance, he will not stop loving them. And he will comfort you. You are not to blame. The pull of the sinful world and enemy are to blame. Fight for your child with love and kindness, lots of prayers, and by living out a life wrapped in Jesus for them to see. Don't give up hope!

REFLECTIONS

- Has one of your adult children (or someone's child who you know) turned their back on God? Have you struggled with blame or guilt about the situation? What other emotions does this bring out in you? How have you handled your child's decision? How can you continue to show unconditional love to your child throughout their journey?
- What "work" are you doing now for your child's relationship with God? Obviously, we as parents can't earn our children's salvation, but we can certainly continue to fight the enemy with God's Word and our prayers that they be brought back into the light. How can you make sure your child sees Jesus in you each day?
- What Scriptures do you pray over your child? What helps you stand firm against the enemy's attacks? How have you seen God's strength at work to get you through the weeping?

PRAYER

God, Your Word says you left the 99 to find the one.
Will you please pursue my child and bring them
back into your fold? Thank you, Jesus. Amen.

All the Feels of Frustration

"I have told you these things, so that in me you may
have peace. In this world you will have trouble. But
take heart! I have overcome the world."

JOHN 16:33 (NIV)

My youngest, Jessica, began to stutter shortly before she turned three. The harder she tried to say a word, the more frustrated she became. Sometimes a distraction would calm her, and she'd reply, without stammering, "I just can't say that word."

Fortunately, a colleague from my teaching days, a speech therapist, gave me tips to help Jessica alleviate her frustrations. "Most kids outgrow stuttering on their own," she added.

Wouldn't it be great if we could outgrow all of our frustrations? Life gets in the way, though, and frustrations seem to occur often for busy moms. When I am anxious, I get frustrated easily. When things don't go my way, when the world seems so cruel and heartless, when my necklace tangles for the umpteenth time and I'm in a hurry to leave the house, when I've repeatedly made the same correction for one child or fought the same battle of "I don't want this for dinner" with another child.

God warned us about troubles and that means plenty of frustrations! But those frustrations don't have to wreck our day. God promises peace. True peace comes from the heavenly Father, the Creator AND

Overcomer of the world. He's already won every battle, every war—and he has conquered *every single frustration*! Take a deep breath, reach for him, and cling to his perfect peace.

REFLECTIONS

- What circumstances seem to frustrate you easily? What frustrates you about the daily tasks of being a mom? How do you typically handle minor frustrations? What about major ones? Do you think you could handle frustrations and irritations in a better way? What are practical steps that you can take that will help you work through frustrations better?

- What does it mean to you to "have peace"? What does a "peaceful day" look like to you? How can you wrap your head around the idea that God promises peace to those who call on his name and lean into him?

- Do you truly believe that God has overcome the world? If the answer is no, what would it take for you to believe those words? How does that belief change the way you face minor (and major) frustrations in a typical mom-day?

PRAYER

Dear God, empower me with your peace and give me strength to withstand the little frustrations and the huge ones, too. Thank you for already overcoming the world and every single battle I'll face. Amen.

Conquering Self-Doubt

I can do all things through Christ who strengthens me.
PHILIPPIANS 4:13 (NKJV)

Siv and her husband looked forward to their first foster placement, three sisters five-years-old and younger. "I'm finally a mom," Siv said, "at least temporarily for now." Tantrums and tears later—some the girls' and some hers—along with challenges with the case worker, the system, and the biological mom, made Siv doubt her abilities. Could she really be a mom for the precious girls?

"I don't think I'm cut out for this after all," she whispered to her husband one night.

Just before bedtime, the middle sister handed Siv a piece of paper illustrated with five disproportionate stick figures. "It's our family," she announced. "And this is you." Her chubby finger pointed to one of the characters on the page. Siv hugged her tightly, kissed her forehead, and tucked her into bed with happy teardrops dampening the pillow.

Self-doubts about motherhood often lurk around the corner, waiting to pounce whenever a situation gives easy passage to negative thoughts. Doubts and questions occur with new moms, as well as seasoned moms entering a new stage or childhood phase. It happens. The enemy likes to whisper we can't handle this or that aspect of mothering. The best counterattack is to yell or scream right back at the enemy—metaphorically of course—that we *can* handle it—not on our own strength but with the power of Christ who resides within us. We can do ALL stages and phases of motherhood with Christ's help. Don't doubt that promise!

- What situations create a sense of doubt for you? What aspects of motherhood cause you to doubt yourself or your abilities to be a good mom? What helps you overcome those feelings? How have you seen God intervene during moments of doubt? How did he prove himself faithful to his promise of strength?
- What gets in the way of believing today's verse, that you can do ALL things through Christ? How does it change your reaction to self-doubt when you realize that the same power that raised Christ from the dead now resides in you by way of the Holy Spirit?
- When do you find that you need Christ's strength the most? What does it mean to you to lean on his strength and not your own? How can you shift your focus from doubt to his strength instead?

PRAYER

God, sometimes I doubt my abilities. When I get discouraged, help me remember that I can't do this life without you. Give me strength, Lord. Remind me that I CAN mother well through Christ who strengthens me. Amen.

Trust in the Lord, the Rock Eternal

You will keep in perfect peace those whose minds are
steadfast, because they trust in you. Trust in the LORD forever,
for the LORD, the LORD himself, is the Rock eternal.

ISAIAH 26:3-4 (NIV)

Toddler Jeru spiked a fever and Tamika was baffled. Just the day before, the on-call doctor had dismissed his symptoms. Even the neighbor said Tamika was overreacting.

Tamika called her stepmom and shared her concerns. "Mom, he's just not himself. Something's not right."

"Trust your instincts, honey," she said. "You're his mom. You know him best. Doctors are wonderful, but they don't know everything. Pray. Trust your feelings."

When Tamika secured an appointment with Jeru's pediatrician, X-rays revealed pneumonia in both his lungs.

It's hard to know who to trust when parenting our precious treasures. Even those who mean well can sometimes make mistakes. There's One we can trust wholeheartedly. God is our Rock. He doesn't make mistakes—ever. He can be trusted with every detail of our lives. He is faithful, he is just, and he will never fail us. He is worthy of our trust.

Even on days full of discouragement and challenges, he can be trusted. Even on our darkest days, our most difficult days, he can be trusted. We can turn toward his light, and it will always, always be greater than the darkness. When we steadfastly trust in him, he promises to give us peace. Trust him and don't let go. He's your Rock eternal!

- Besides God, who do you trust to help you make wise decisions about your parenting? What helps you know you can trust that person? What in their past and present validates their trustworthiness? Without becoming jaded about humanity, what helps you remember that humans are not infallible—even the well-meaning ones?
- How can you know with all certainty that God is infallible? How has he proved himself perfect and trustworthy in the past? When we recount with thanksgiving and praise the many times he's taken care of us in the past, we remember his goodness, strength, and trustworthiness in the present.
- How can you trust God with an unwavering steadfastness? What can you do afresh each morning that will renew your trust? How can you thank God today for the peace that his trustworthiness brings? How does his peace empower you today?

PRAYER

Dear God, renew my trust in you daily. Give me the peace
that comes with trusting you wholeheartedly so that I
choose wisely those I trust here on earth. Amen.

Holding On to God through Infertility and Miscarriage

Seek the LORD and his strength; seek his presence continually!
1 CHRONICLES 16:11 (ESV)

When Joanie's firstborn turned five years old, Joanie suffered a devastating miscarriage with her next pregnancy. She cried out to the Lord in pain and loss. She tearfully questioned God, but thanked him for his sovereignty.

Several infertile years later, Joanie and her husband became foster-to-adopt parents. Joanie prayed often for the child who might soon join them. Months and lots of paperwork later, the couple adopted a sibling group of four from longtime foster care. God's plans turned out to be much bigger than Joanie ever dreamed.

Infertility and miscarriage can be overwhelming, debilitating losses for women. God catches every tear and stays close to the brokenhearted. He longs to comfort us in our deep place of sorrow. His mighty strength can uphold us, even in our darkest days. When we feel like we can't put one foot in front of the other, his arms around us help us go the distance, one step at a time.

God promises that suffering and brokenness aren't the end. Our loss is never the final word of the story he's writing for our life. Though the pain may last through the night, joy will come in the morning. Morning's light may feel unreachable, but our Father's light is just a whisper away. He's right there next to us. He never leaves.

Seek his strength. Seek his presence. Let his light dispel your darkness. Reach out and grab hold of God and settle into the comfort of his loving arms.

REFLECTIONS

- Have you suffered a devastating loss, like miscarriage or infertility? Are you still in the shadows of that loss? What helps you cope with devastating loss? How do you seek God during trials like this? What helps you feel his presence in the midst of your pain and suffering?
- If you haven't been through a painful loss, who comes to mind who has? How can you offer comfort and help or just your presence?
- It's okay to grieve what we've lost, and God longs to comfort us. How can you seek his strength during a time like this? Can you recall another time of loss when you relied on his strength? How might that memory help you get through this current pain? God knew great loss, too, when his only Son suffered and died on the cross. He understands. Let that comfort you.

PRAYER

God, this loss hurts in big ways. Let me feel your presence through my pain. Thank you that Jesus' death on the cross wasn't the end of the story. I'm thankful for his resurrection and the promise of eternity. Amen.

Confidence to Move Past "Not Good Enough"

He who began a good work in you will carry it on to completion until the day of Christ Jesus.
PHILIPPIANS 1:6 (NIV)

Cheryl's mom called with yet another announcement of Cheryl's half-sister's accomplishments. Cheryl and her older sister were close, but somehow, Candy always outdid her when it came to achievements. Cheryl tried to be happy for Candy, but she found herself comparing more often than celebrating.

"I'll never be good enough to meet my parents' approval," Cheryl told her best friend.

Striving to be good enough is especially challenging when family members are involved. The fact of the matter is, none of us are "good enough" without the blood of Jesus Christ to redeem and sanctify us. But God isn't finished with us yet. He works in us every day to make us more like him, to bear the image of Jesus.

We don't have to compare ourselves to others or attempt to be "good enough" for someone else. Our job is to strive to be more and more like Jesus with every breath, in every action and word and deed, to live in the plans he has for us. The good works that he ordained for us, in us and through us, he promises to bring to completion, one beautiful day at a time, until Jesus returns. When we focus on that promise, it leaves us little time to compare ourselves to others here on earth!

- Do you fight feelings of "not good enough"? To whom do you compare yourself the most? What makes you focus on that particular relationship (or relationships)? What can you do to move past those feelings? If someone in your family has made you feel "less than," whether deliberately or inadvertently, how can you work through that to have a healthier attitude toward your own worth?
- Do you believe God has a "good work" planned for your life? I hope you said yes to that rhetorical question! With that recognition, how can you face each day with a new sense of worth and value?
- What distracts you from recognizing God's lavish and unfailing love? How can you make a daily habit of praising him for his love and learn to measure your worth according to that love instead of comparing yourself to others?

PRAYER

God, help me tune out the "not good enough" whispers. Help me hear your reminders that it's you who finishes the good work in me. Amen.

When Dreams Go Unfulfilled

But as for me, I watch in hope for the LORD, I wait
for God my Savior; my God will hear me.

MICAH 7:7 (NIV)

Zoey longed for a partner to share life and parenting responsibilities with. She expressed her desires to longtime friend and stay-at-home mom, Shannon.

Shannon responded, "You know, Zoey, you're living the life I've always dreamed of. A successful career and healthy, well-adjusted children. I love my kids, but I want to have a career one day, too."

Zoey said, "Well, I guess I could say the same about your life. I pray for God to send someone I can grow old with. You're living my dream, Shannon! Sometimes, I wonder if God even hears me."

Have you ever felt that way? That God doesn't hear your prayers about an unfulfilled dream? I don't profess to understand his ways at all times, but I believe with my whole heart that he hears us and that he is always good, no matter what circumstance troubles us.

God wants what is best for us. Whatever he allows, however he chooses to act or answer, we can rest assured that ultimately, he makes ALL things work together for our good. Individual circumstances may not feel good—and may be really hard—but he works through all these situations to make us stronger, draw us closer to him, and show us his love and glory.

Don't give up on your dream. Tell God all about it and wait in hope. He loves you dearly. He hears you.

REFLECTIONS

- What unmet desire do you have? Have you talked to God about your unfulfilled dream? Do you tell him your concerns often? What do you think is holding you back from "living the dream" you desire? Is it something you can work on or will it take a miracle from God? How often do you pray expectantly for that miracle?
- What does it mean to you to "watch in hope for the LORD" in Micah 7:7 (NIV)? How can you grow closer to him while you wait?
- How can you be assured that God hears your prayers? Recall times in the past when God heard and answered your prayers. How can these memories give you confidence to know God always hears you? List as many answered prayers as you can think of. Add to the list periodically as a reminder of God's faithfulness.

PRAYER

God, you know my heart and my unfulfilled dreams. Help me wait for you with confidence that you hear my every prayer. Amen.

Don't Believe the Enemy's Lies

The thief comes only to steal and kill and destroy. I came
that they may have life and have it abundantly.

JOHN 10:10 (ESV)

When Chrissy shared a picture of her strong-willed, rambunctious middle schooler on social media, a stranger posted unkind comments about her parenting abilities. The cruel remarks reminded her of an earlier time when a family member judged her parenting skills with disdain and negativity. "I'm a terrible mom," she thought. "Maybe I don't deserve this happiness."

Unfortunately for humankind, the enemy whispers lies to make us doubt our worth and value, seeking to destroy lives and relationships. The darkness left behind inflicts guilt and evokes sadness and regret, stealing our joy and robbing us of our happiness.

Jesus came to earth as God in the flesh to shine light into the darkness. His light dispels the darkness and gives us hope. God loves us so deeply that he sent his only Son to die on the cross so that we might live. He wants us to live life to the fullest. With his lavish love poured out on us, we can live abundantly. Will life be perfect and free from pain? Definitely not, but he promises never to leave us or forsake us. We can live with joy and happiness, contentment and gratefulness. He loves us deeper and wider than we can even fathom.

Don't believe the lies. Rejoice in God's love instead, and live the abundant life God wants for you.

REFLECTIONS

- What lies has the enemy whispered to you recently? What helps you stand up to those lies and stand firm when facing the adversary?
- What does "abundant life" look like to you? Remember, abundant doesn't mean easy or pain-free or lacking troubles. Abundant *does* mean wrapped in the arms of God. Consumed with the love of Jesus. And filled with the Holy Spirit. It doesn't get any better!
- Who do you know who lives an "abundant life" with God? What practices or character traits does that person have that you'd like to emulate? What do they do each day that reflects their close walk with God? What if you truly believed that God wanted to give you an abundant life? How might each day look different for you?

PRAYER

Father, help me not to believe the lies of the enemy.
Give me an abundant life. Help me seek you always.
Thank you for loving me so well. Amen.

Overcome with Exhaustion? Rest in the Lord!

The LORD replied, "My Presence will go with
you, and I will give you rest."
EXODUS 33:14 (NIV)

Trucilla picked up her three-year-old twin boys from daycare. "Let's go
get your sister from school now." Absentmindedly listening to their chat-
ter, Trucilla reviewed the rest of her afternoon: karate lessons, grocery
store for milk, something—what?—for dinner, Wednesday night church
activities, bath time, bedtime stories, at least a few minutes spent with
her husband, and emails to prepare for tomorrow's meeting.

She was exhausted just thinking about the few short hours before
bedtime. When she told the twins about the grocery store run, Jackson
said, "I know idea, Mommy. Let's eat cereal for dinner."

"You know sweetie, I think that's the best idea anyone's had all day!"

Mom fatigue and burnout are real! So many responsibilities. God
sees our distress and promises rest. We only need to reach out to him.
Simply coming into God's presence gives us physical, mental, and spiri-
tual rest. When we pour out our heart to him, giving him our cares and
burdens, he quiets our minds, allowing us to rest peacefully with the
comfort of knowing we're not alone. A daily relationship with him gives
us the confidence that he'll never leave us or forsake us.

When we put our faith and trust in Jesus, we're promised the forgiveness of sins and the blessing of eternal life. We can rest in our salvation. His presence gives us rest that leads to peace. Mom fatigue may reign for a season, but God is King for eternity.

REFLECTIONS

- How often do you find yourself flopping into bed at night, overcome with fatigue? Though it may not seem helpful at this very moment, keep in mind that the season you're in will not last forever. Take a deep breath, hang on to God, and walk forward one day at a time.
- What steps can you take to let go of some responsibilities during this busy season of motherhood? Who can you reach out to for help? How can you make sure to treasure these mommy-days and not miss out on making memories while keeping your sanity at the same time?
- In this moment, how can you seek God's presence that will make all the difference in how you face the day's challenges? What helps you know with certainty that God is always with you? How can you rely on God's strength to help you bear today's responsibilities?

PRAYER

God, I'm tired. Please give me rest. Help me rely on your strength each day. Thank you for your presence. I can't do this without you. Amen.

Practice Patience with Perseverance and Prayers

Let your hope make you glad. Be patient in time of trouble and never stop praying.
ROMANS 12:12 (CEV)

Stefani braked and mumbled under her breath. "This darn light will make me late for work again."

Four-year-old Brenda responded from her car seat, "Don't get mad, Mommy. The yellow light just wants to keep you safe."

Stefani smiled at Brenda in the rearview mirror and said, "You're right, honey. And maybe Mommy needs to practice patience today."

How do you feel about practicing patience? I learned a long time ago not to pray for patience, because then God gives me opportunities to practice. I'm kidding, of course, but patience doesn't come easily for me. And I often seem to lose patience more easily over little irritations than I do with big challenges. It's as if my heart immediately defaults to God's help when I face a huge challenge, but those seemingly insignificant ones, my brain attempts to handle on my own strength and power. I usually fail miserably, too.

When will I learn that I can do nothing on my own power? I need God's strength for little trials, big difficulties, and everything in-between. Persistent prayers keep me in a right relationship with the

Lord. Persevering with hope makes my heart happy. And practicing patience requires a close proximity to God to keep me from failing daily.

We can only master patience with help from the Holy Spirit. Growing in patience makes us more Christ-like. How's your patience today?

REFLECTIONS

- Can you name the fruit of the Spirit without looking at Galatians 5:22–23? I'll help—love, joy, peace, patience, kindness, goodness, faithfulness, gentleness, and self-control. Which one of these attributes do you struggle with the most? Is patience near the top of your list? How do you actively work to show forth the fruit of the Spirit in your daily walk with God?
- Do you lack patience more often with minor irritations or major catastrophes? How do you respond when impatience takes over? In what way do you want to change that reaction?
- How can you "be patient in time of trouble and never stop praying" (Romans 12:12 CEV)? What steps can you take to practice patience? What does your day look like when you "pray without ceasing"? Who do you know who exhibits patience readily? What do you think makes that person patient?

PRAYER

Dear God, patience is not easy for me. Help me rely on your strength, through prayers and the promise of hope, to be more patient. Thank you for extending patience to me! Amen.

Take Hold of My Hand, God—I Need Your Help

"For I am the LORD your God who takes hold of your right hand, Who says to you, 'Do not fear, I will help you.'"

ISAIAH 41:13 (NASB)

Kennita's husband lost his job and struggled to find another one. "Everyone wants to hire the younger generation," he told Kennita.

"We'll make do on my salary until you find something, babe," Kennita said, but silently wondered how they'd pay high school senior graduation fees, help their college student with dorm expenses, and buy a baby gift for a soon-to-be-born grandchild. Not to mention make payments on a much-needed used car now that her husband wouldn't be walking to work.

Kennita and Corliss prayed diligently and asked friends to pray, too. Weeks went by without a job prospect. One afternoon, Kennita received a phone call from someone at church. An anonymous donor wanted to gift the couple a used car. Both wept with appreciation and thanked God for answered prayers.

If you're facing financial problems, God promises to help you. You may not receive a car with no strings attached like Kennita and Corliss, but God will see you through the struggle. God promises to take care of all of our needs. He sometimes uses others to supply those needs—friends, family, or random strangers. He may give us the creativity to provide for our own needs. He just might work a miracle to alleviate our financial woes.

Answers may not come right away, but take hold of God's hand and let go of fear. God will help you.

REFLECTIONS

- Are you currently facing financial difficulties? Are you dealing with other challenges that you don't know how to handle? What about today's verse can help you trust God to supply all your needs? What do you need most from the Lord today?

- When fear waits for us around every corner, we're threatened with a debilitating darkness. But our circumstances don't catch God by surprise. Even if our situation never changes, God is still good. His light shines bright in the darkness. How can you reach out to God and grab hold of his light and love?

- Our suffering doesn't define us, nor is it the end of our story. But it can help us grow stronger when we trust God rather than fear our circumstances. What do you fear most today? How can you turn those fears over to God and trust his promise of help?

PRAYER

God, when fears come crashing in, show me how to trust you. Give me the strength to face every circumstance. Thank you for helping me. Amen.

Sweep Away My Failures and Remember Them No More

"I am the one, I sweep away your transgressions for
my own sake and remember your sins no more."
ISAIAH 43:25 (CSB)

Genevieve served 18 months in prison for embezzling money from her workplace. She told a counselor upon release that she didn't know how to face friends and family again. "I lost time with my teenagers that I'll never get back," she said. "I know they're embarrassed. I can't even forgive myself, so I don't think God ever will, either."

Do you have failures that you think are too big for God to forgive? No mistake is so messy that he can't sweep away the transgression and remember it no more. God loves us with such intensity that he sent his own Son to earth to die a miserable death so that our sins could be covered by the blood of Jesus Christ. If he loves us that much, no sin, mistake, or failure will hinder his forgiveness.

Forgiveness surrounds us because of Jesus' death on the cross, and hope for eternity abounds because of an empty grave. We only need to ask. God's lavish love spills over onto us daily, with mercies anew every morning.

The enemy wants us to wallow in guilt and shame. He wants us to feel unworthy. Don't let the evil one succeed. Jesus triumphed on the cross when he said, "It is finished." Welcome his forgiveness. Practice forgiving yourself. Learn from your mistakes and failures and draw closer to him along the way.

- What mistakes and failures do you regret? Have you earnestly sought forgiveness from God? God promises to remember our sins no more! What keeps you from believing that promise of today's verse?
- In 2 Corinthians 5:17, we are reminded that accepting Jesus as our Savior makes us a new creation—the old "us" is gone and a new creation has come. How did your life change when you became a believer? What are some big differences in the "old" you and the "new" you? What about minor changes? What areas of your life do you need to continue working on, with God's help, to make you more like Jesus? Put on your "new self" each day!
- What lessons have you learned from past mistakes? How have you used these failures to help you grow closer to God? What battle plan can you initiate to fight the enemy's attacks of shame and guilt?

PRAYER

God, forgive me of past, present, and future sins. Thank you for the gift of forgiveness. Remind me that you never stop renewing me. Amen.

Give God Your Burdens

Cast your cares on the LORD and he will sustain you.
PSALM 55:22 (NIV)

Just shy of his first birthday, Keith received a neuromuscular disorder diagnosis when his mom, Samantha, questioned the pediatrician about Keith's gross motor development. Samantha had consistently noticed differences in Keith's development as compared to that of his two older siblings. Devastated, confused, and at a loss for how to handle his care, Samantha prayed, asking God for a miracle for Keith.

Several weeks later, a family moved into Samantha's neighborhood. When she delivered homemade cookies to introduce herself, Samantha found out the new couple's six-year-old son had the same disorder as Keith. The women bonded immediately and made plans for an upcoming playdate for the kids. "I think I just got the miracle I've prayed for," Samantha thought as she walked back home.

What cares are burdening your heart today? A special needs or sick child? Loneliness? An empty nest season? Financial woes? Elderly parents? Loss of employment? An unruly teenager?

As long as this earth spins, we will face troubles. Sometimes daily; sometimes not. Oftentimes huge problems; many times small annoyances. God sees us. He knows what plagues us. He longs to comfort and sustain us. God will never leave us or forsake us. He's always within our reach. He hears every prayer and catches every tear.

Whatever is bothering you today, my friend, give your cares to him. Nothing is too big for him, and nothing is too trivial. He can handle it all. He wants to help you.

- Do you truly believe God is big enough to handle your huge burdens? How do you "cast" your cares on him? Do you ever feel like your problems are too insignificant to talk to God about? What can you do to get past that feeling? For example, you might consider some of God's "little" creations. If God cares about all the intricate details of small insects, don't you think he is concerned about the details of your life too?
- What burden are you carrying right now? What problem are you facing that you don't have an answer for? How can you release that burden into God's hands and care?
- Think back to another time when you faced a significant burden or problem. How did God take you through that situation? How can that help you trust God in full expectancy that he will get you through this challenge as well?

PRAYER

God, I don't know how to handle what I'm facing, but I know that you can. Sustain me with your strength. I put my trust in you. Amen.

Nothing's Too Hard for God

"O Sovereign LORD! You made the heavens and earth by your strong hand and powerful arm. Nothing is too hard for you!"

JEREMIAH 32:17 (NLT)

"You're not my mother. You can't tell me what to do." Becky slammed her bedroom door.

Will I ever succeed in this stepparenting role, Lord? It's just too hard! Anika had reminded Becky to finish her homework assignments before walking to the skate park with her friends.

Hours later, Becky burst through the front door—homework completed first—with four friends tagging along behind her. "Mom, will you help my friends and I make cookies? You make the BEST oatmeal cookies ever!"

"Me," Anika corrected with a smile. "Will you help my friends and *me* make cookies, and of course I will. You grab the eggs and butter; I'll get the other ingredients."

Are you dealing with something that feels way too hard to accomplish? A stepparenting role? A troubled marriage? A difficult college assignment? A prodigal child? An insufferable employer?

The very Creator of the world is just a whisper away when you need him! He wants you to call on him for everything. Reach out and grab hold of his strong hand and don't let go. Nothing is too hard for him and he will see you through.

Will your situation change immediately? Most likely not, but you can trust that he will sustain you with his strength and carry you through to the end, whatever that may look like. Lean into his strength and power. He's got you!

REFLECTIONS

- What hard circumstance are you facing? What is your default response when something is more than you can bear? Do you share your concerns with God and turn it over to him?
- Do you keep a record of answered prayers? Consider keeping a journal or notebook of prayer requests and answers. Write dates beside the entries to serve as reminders of God's faithfulness. Is there something you've prayed about for months or maybe years? Don't give up. Share your concerns with God. He hears every word and is working all things together for your good, even when everything around you seems counter to that promise.
- How can you believe with conviction that "nothing is too hard for God?" How different might your prayers sound if you truly believed that statement? How will your reactions and responses change when you believe the truth of Jeremiah 32:17?

PRAYER

God, thank you that nothing is too hard for you. When I try to tackle a problem on my own, help me rely on your strength instead. Amen.

Trusting God in Times of Uncertainty

The LORD is good, a refuge in times of trouble.
He cares for those who trust in him.

NAHUM 1:7 (NIV)

After years of verbal cruelty that escalated into physical abuse and unfaithfulness, Sofia stepped away from her marriage to protect her children. When she filed for divorce, her husband threatened to seek full custody of the kids.

The uncertainty of her situation terrified Sofia, but, armed with evidence and surrounded by supportive family and friends, she trusted God to get her and the kids through it.

The troubles of this world create dark shadows of uncertainty that only the light of God can dispel. No matter what our situation, no matter how difficult the task, no matter how gloomy the outcome, no matter how devastating the tragedy, God is still good! He will always, always be good. Nothing ever changes or takes away his goodness. The circumstances may not be good, but God is.

We can take refuge in his strength. We don't have to stay in the shadows of darkness. We can take shelter instead in the shadow of his wings, surrounded by his light. God will care for us. We can trust and believe that he will fight the battles for us. He will carry us through whatever dark, troubling situation we're facing. Darkness is part of this life, but his light will always overcome it.

No matter how dire the situation seems to us, God is right there beside us, not only protecting us but fighting for us as well. His goodness will prevail in times of uncertainty!

- What uncertainty are you facing? Who do you turn to in times of uncertainty? Who, besides God, has your back during troubling times? What answer to prayer do you need to turn your situation around? Are you seeking God for that answer?
- What uncertain times have you encountered in the past? How did God protect you and fight for you then? In what specific ways could you clearly see his hand in every detail of the situation? How have you used that situation to encourage and support someone else during their time of uncertainty?
- Make a list of God's good qualities. Then, close your eyes for a minute and picture yourself taking refuge in the shadow of God. Embrace his refuge and protection. What does it feel like? How does that help you put your trust in him? How can you trust him more deeply in times of uncertainty?

PRAYER

God, help me trust you in times of uncertainty. You are good—so good—all the time, and I'm grateful for that. I love you, Lord. Amen.

When the Nest is Empty

"And be sure of this: I am with you always, even to the end of the age."

MATTHEW 28:20 (NLT)

"I just don't know what to do with these long, lonely days," Irene told Aubrey. "I've only been a mom my whole adult life. Now that all the kids have moved away, I have nothing to keep me busy. I don't have the education, skills, or experience to join the workforce at my age or to even volunteer."

"You know what, Irene? I've got a great plan for you. Here's something you can do until you figure out the next step." Aubrey told Irene about an organization that collects handmade blankets for the homeless. Aubrey knew that her stay-at-home mom friend had made dozens of baby blankets as gifts when their kids were little.

"Great idea, Aubrey! And that way, I'll still feel like I'm taking care of someone."

Loneliness often accompanies different stages of motherhood. First-time moms. Stay-at-home moms. Moms of busy teens. And empty-nest moms.

But one thing's for certain: we are never truly alone, because Jesus promises us in Matthew 28:20 that he is with us from now until eternity. God reminds us a number of times throughout the Bible that he will "never leave us nor forsake us." God never slumbers or sleeps, therefore he is with us around the clock, every day of the week, throughout the calendar for this year, and for all of eternity. Does that comfort you as much as it comforts me?

- Have you gone through a season of loneliness during different stages of motherhood? Are you in an empty-nest season currently? If your answer is no, do you have a friend or family member in a lonely season? What can you do for yourself or someone else to alleviate the depressing feelings of loneliness?
- Perhaps your current season isn't one of loneliness, but revolves around a major lifestyle change. Are you struggling to find a new purpose or different path to follow? How does it comfort you to know that God is with you, wherever that path leads? How might you find a way to serve others during this season of life change?
- In what circumstances in the past have you felt God's presence? What helps you feel his presence most vividly? Prayer time? Worship music? A nature walk? How can you incorporate more activities that help you feel close to God?

PRAYER

Dear God, thank you that you're always with me, in the past, as well as from now until eternity. I don't want to walk this path without you. Amen.

When We Feel Like We're Not Enough

See what great love the Father has lavished on us,
that we should be called children of God!

1 JOHN 3:1 (NIV)

Isabelle's heart began to race one night when she realized she'd signed up to provide a cake for the middle school party the very next day. Rummaging through the pantry, the only thing she found was an unopened box of gluten-free chocolate chip cookies.

All day at work, Isabelle fretted over her failure. "It just feels like I'm never enough," she told her husband on the phone.

When Ramona came home from school, Isabelle apologized again for forgetting the cake.

"No worries, Momma. A couple of kids in my class have gluten allergies like you, and our cookies were the only gluten-free dessert there. They loved it! Thanks, Momma."

Failures and mistakes sometimes cause us moms to feel inadequate, like we're not enough. When those insecurities kick in, it helps to remember that we walk in the light of God's love. Whatever we think we lack, God is more than enough to compensate for our shortcomings. Whenever we think, "I'm not," God reminds us: "I AM." He loves us with such a lavish love that we need not feel lacking or inadequate in any area. Nothing we do (or don't do) will ever change God's love for us. He calls us his children, and he loves us with an everlasting love.

Whenever you feel inadequate or "not enough," wrap your mind and heart around the truth that you are loved lavishly by your heavenly Father. Let his arms hold you tight until you feel more than enough!

REFLECTIONS

- What situations make you feel like you're "not enough"? Has anyone ever suggested that you're "not enough" or do you impose those feelings on yourself? Why do you think you harbor those insecurities? Is there something you can do today that will help you feel worthy? For example, memorize today's verse, and whenever insecurities threaten your mind, recite the verse over and over until you feel God's love pouring over you.
- What does the verb "lavish" mean to you? Look up other translations of 1 John 3:1 and write them on notecards. Then rewrite the NIV translation, replacing the word "lavished" with these synonyms: heaped, showered, poured, deluged, gushed, teemed, and flooded. With that kind of love slathered on us, how can we feel inadequate or unworthy?
- What's your favorite part about being a child of God? How can you thank God today for being a good, good Father?

PRAYER

God, when I feel like I'm not enough, remind me that your love makes me more than enough. I'm glad I'm your child. Amen.

Trust in the Lord and Soar

But those who trust in the LORD will find new strength.
They will soar high on wings like eagles. They will run
and not grow weary. They will walk and not faint.

ISAIAH 40:31 (NLT)

When Lauren pointed out a new lump to her doctor, an imaging appointment confirmed her fears—breast cancer. Words like lumpectomy, chemotherapy, radiation, and reconstructive surgery clouded her brain.

The cancer specialist offered comfort and assurance but no guarantees. Before surgery, Lauren told her teenage kids, "The God I serve will deliver me from breast cancer. But if not . . . I will still praise him."

Have you ever encountered a life-threatening illness? Has someone close to you received devastating news? This life is hard, especially when a cancer diagnosis or fatal illness affects someone we love. Or, when a different kind of devastating blow comes out of nowhere, like a job loss, accidental death of a child, the breakup of a longtime marriage, or betrayal from someone close.

God sees these devastating occurrences. He didn't cause them, but for whatever reason, he allows them. We may never know this side of heaven why bad things happen to good people, but we can trust that God remains good. When we trust him completely and give him our weaknesses, we find new strength in him. We can soar, despite our circumstances. We can run and not grow weary, regardless of our situations. We can trust him to get us through whatever lies before us in ways that will glorify him, because he is good.

- What life-threatening situations have you or someone you love faced? What helped you get through the difficulties of that situation? How did you persevere through devastating circumstances? What helped you feel God's presence during that time?
- What is the most difficult part of trusting God? When your trust starts to waver during a tragic circumstance, how can you get back on track, trusting him with your whole heart? Who can you reach out to who can keep you accountable in your walk with God during a tragedy or difficult diagnosis?
- What do you need God's strength for today? Be specific with your answers. Ask God for strength with each detail, no matter how big or trivial. Let him help you walk through each trial, run through each challenge, and soar through each situation. Lean on his strength. He's got you! Trust him!

PRAYER

God, this situation is scary. I don't know the outcome, but I know I'm not alone. Let me rest in your strength. Keep me from growing weary. Help me soar high with you! Amen.

Let God Be Your Fortress

The LORD is my light and my salvation; whom shall I fear? The
LORD is the stronghold of my life; of whom shall I be afraid?
PSALM 27:1 (ESV)

Alyssa never believed it could happen in her small town, but someone
kidnapped two children from a nearby neighborhood. Weeks later, offi-
cers found their bodies. Traumatized, many in the community, including
Alyssa, became overzealous in protecting their children.

Whenever her kids were out of sight, Alyssa felt as if she were having a panic attack. Anxiety riddled her every thought and action. It took
quite some time, and help from a therapist, but Alyssa learned to redirect her thoughts and calm her fears.

Whether caused by actual events or our own flawed perceptions,
fears can devastate us and prevent us from being the strong mommas
that we need to be. Fear keeps us enslaved to the "what-ifs" of the world.

Christ came to take away our fears, to give us peace. Jesus said in
John 14:27 (NIV), "Peace I leave with you; my peace I give you. I do not
give to you as the world gives. Do not let your hearts be troubled and do
not be afraid."

God is our light and salvation. His light is far more powerful than
the darkness of the world. When we walk in his light and turn our fears,
real or perceived, over to him, we can have peace. Scary circumstances

will still take place in the world, but with God as our strength and stronghold, we can live without fear.

REFLECTIONS

- What do you fear most as a mommy? How do you keep a handle on those fears to prevent anxiety or irrational behavior? In what ways does fear keep you from being the mom, wife, daughter, or friend you want to be? What can you do to change that? Do you think a Christian counselor could help you work through your fears?
- Think about various sources of light for a moment. Like the sun, a bright lamp, a flashlight, a car's headlights, a glowing candle. What does each of those do to the darkness? In what ways can you think of the Lord as your light, dispelling your darkest fears and worries? Walk in his light daily.
- Look up the word "stronghold" and you'll see words like "fortified," "protected," and "upheld." Describe how God is the "stronghold" of your life. How can that definition alleviate your fears?

PRAYER

Dear God, when I'm afraid, help me turn to you. You are my salvation and my stronghold. Fortify me with your love and hold me in your strong arms. Amen.

Prioritizing Relationships with the Adults in Our Lives

Beloved, let us love one another, for love is of God; and everyone who loves is born of God and knows God.

1 JOHN 4:7 (NKJV)

"Why didn't you tell me you had a work trip this weekend?" Sheila asked her husband. "I have a virtual meeting, and I have to finish that big presentation. I was counting on your help with the kids."

"I did tell you, honey. You wrote it in your calendar."

"I barely have time to check my calendar, and you're always working," Sheila answered. "We've got to do something about our communication."

Moms, as important as our kids are, our relationships with the significant adults in our lives are vitally important, too. For our mental health and social well-being, we need to find time for these adults we value and treasure. Making time for a spouse, family member, or significant other takes intentionality. Prioritizing adult relationships takes effort. You may need to get creative to spend quality time together. And communication is key to building a firm foundation based on love.

Loving others well is biblical. God commands us to love one another. We have the capability to love others because love comes from God. In 1 John 4:19 (NIV) it says, "We love because he first loved us."

Showing love to the important adults in our lives helps our children learn to love well too, and teaches them the value of family. And most importantly, it gives them a glimpse of the lavish love of their heavenly Father.

- Aside from your children (and God, of course), who are the most significant people in your life? In what ways do you show love to these adults? Do you know the love language of each of these important people? Do they know your love language?
- What can you do to spend more quality time with your spouse (or other significant person)? How can you be intentional to spend uninterrupted time with your special person? How does a better relationship with your spouse help you be a better mother?
- What's one thing you can do today that will improve communication with your spouse? When's the last time you surprised your spouse with a card, note, date, or weekend getaway? How often do you express your love and appreciation to your spouse? How does knowing God help you love others better?

PRAYER

God, help me love others well, especially the significant adults in my life. Thank you for loving me with an everlasting, unconditional love. Thank you for teaching me how to love. I love you, God. Amen.

Take Anxious Thoughts Captive and Give Your Worries to God

Give all your worries and cares to God, for he cares about you.

1 PETER 5:7 (NLT)

With her mom sitting right next to her in the upstairs playroom, toddler Hailey slipped on a toy, landing with a thud on the floor. Hailey wailed and cradled her left arm. Parenting solo because her husband was away for work, Linda grabbed a diaper bag and her purse and rushed to the hospital emergency room.

Several hours, a fractured distal radius, and a plaster cast later, Linda drove her sleeping daughter home. Though Hailey's wrist healed perfectly, Linda struggled with anxiety each time her husband traveled again for work. "I have these fears that something terrible is going to happen while he's away," Linda said.

Anxiety cases are rising at a startling rate across the nation, and sometimes, depression accompanies anxiety. If you're struggling with mental health issues, talk with a trusted counselor or pastor and seek help from a medical professional. Please don't ignore signs and symptoms of mental health issues.

My friend, God wants you to give him your worries, concerns, cares, and anxious thoughts. The moment anxiety starts creeping in, pray! God is there. He'll hear your whispered cries for help. Lean into his strength. Keep this verse in mind: "God is our refuge and strength, an ever-present help in trouble" (Psalm 46:1 NIV). He never leaves us. God is our source of strength. Let him empower you to face whatever comes your way. He cares about you, yesterday, today, and tomorrow. He loves you so!

- What concerns are you facing today? After praying about your anxiety, talking with a mental health professional, and sharing your concerns with a trusted family member or friend, what other practical steps can you take to alleviate anxiety? Have your tried taking slow, deep breaths? Is there a technique that helps you refocus to take your mind off of whatever is causing the anxious thoughts?
- Recall a specific time you felt anxious in the past. How did God get you through that situation? How can you use that remembrance in the future to help you rely on God's strength?
- What causes you the most concern about being a mom? Are those concerns warranted from an actual incident or are they "what-if" kinds of thoughts? How can you train your brain to avoid the "what-if" thoughts? How can you learn to take those thoughts captive and give the concerns to God instead?

PRAYER

God, help me give every worry and concern to you. Calm
my anxieties. Be my refuge and strength. Amen.

Facing Fear of Failure

My flesh and my heart may fail, but God is the
strength of my heart and my portion forever.

PSALM 73:26 (NIV)

After spending years as a stay-at-home mom to three children, Lissa
prepared for her first day at work outside the home in almost a decade.
"What if I can't handle the job," she said to her husband. "What if I mess
up—what if I fail?"

In taking on the responsibility of raising another human being,
moms often struggle with the fear of failure. But you know what? Failure
is a fact of life! We're bound to make mistakes. We "mess up" often, and
that's why we need Jesus! Once we admit we are a sinner, believe that
Jesus is God's Son, and confess that he is Lord of our life, our mistakes
and failures and sins are wiped clean. We are forgiven and made new.

No matter how many times we fail or mess up, God never stops loving us. We will always be his children. God is our stronghold forever.
Our bodies will eventually grow old and weak, but God will always be
our heavenly Father. He's all we need for the rest of our lives.

Have you trusted Jesus as your Savior? Have you asked him to be
Lord of your life? Have you given your heart to him? Though we will
make mistakes—and even face failures—and though our bodies will age

and decline, God remains our strength and portion. Don't you want eternity with him?

- Are you afraid of failure? Does it bother you to make mistakes? Who do you worry about failing the most? Children? Spouse? Mom or Dad? Employer? When you make a mistake inadvertently, how do you resolve that mistake? When you fail someone because of a careless mistake, how do you fix that situation?
- Have you accepted Jesus as Savior? What changed when you committed your life to God? What repeated failures do you need to work on? What other hang-ups do you need to address to become more like Jesus? Have you sought forgiveness for your failures?
- Do you tell others about Jesus and the gift of salvation? What excites you the most about eternity with God in heaven? Have you shared that excitement with family and friends who don't know Jesus? Does your life reflect Jesus each day?

PRAYER

God, forgive me when I mess up. Help me forgive myself when I fail. Please give me the strength to move past my mistakes. Thank you for the gift of eternity. Amen.

WEEK 47

Put Your Trust in the One Who Makes You Worthy

Trust in the LORD with all your heart, And lean not on your own understanding; In all your ways acknowledge Him, And He shall direct your paths.

PROVERBS 3:5–6 (NKJV)

Sasha dropped out of college when she got pregnant, which meant she lost her university job and source of income. She was embarrassed to tell her professional-minded, academic parents about her plight. Morning sickness and lack of education limited her work options, and she soon found an eviction notice on her door.

Abandoned by her boyfriend, she felt sure her parents would consider her unworthy as well. Sasha wept unabashed tears when her parents welcomed her home with loving, open arms.

Mistakes, sins, mishaps, and any other grievous, perceived disappointments in ourselves often bring on a feeling of unworthiness. As sinners, each one of us is unworthy without the blood of Jesus to cover our transgressions and sins. However, that does not make us worthless to God. We may not understand why God allows certain things to happen in our lives, and we may not totally grasp the consequences of our sins, but we are never worthless to our Father who loves us more than we can fathom!

When you can't find your way, when you feel worthless in others' eyes, when you don't know which direction to go next, trust the God who will never stop loving you. Take baby steps if you must, but walk forward, and he will direct your path. When you don't understand, trust him. He's walking right beside you, and he will always welcome you home.

REFLECTIONS

- When's the last time you disappointed someone you care for greatly? What circumstances make you feel worthless? Does that feeling arise because of others' words or actions or is your unworthiness a self-imposed feeling?

- How can you push back the enemy's lies about your unworthiness? What can you do to know wholeheartedly that you are worthy because of Jesus' sacrifice on the cross? What verses can you read, record, and memorize to know that you are forgiven, worthy, and loved by the heavenly Father?

- What is your first reaction when you don't understand a life situation or season? How can you acknowledge God during those circumstances? How can those times help you learn to trust God more deeply? On what past life paths have you felt directed by God? How can these memories of God's faithfulness help you in a season of uncertainty?

PRAYER

God, when the path in front of me seems foggy and blurred, be my strength and guide me to walk in your will and way. Thank you for Jesus, who makes me worthy in your eyes. Amen.

Face the Future Unafraid

"The LORD himself goes before you and will be with you; he will never leave you nor forsake you. Do not be afraid; do not be discouraged."

DEUTERONOMY 31:8 (NIV)

Monti fought back tears in the courtroom, only to release them like a dam bursting, later when she climbed into the car alone. Alone. Her new status. With divorce papers in hand, she felt terrified to face the future. "How can I raise my children on my own?" she confided to a friend. "I'm scared I can't support them on my paycheck. It wasn't supposed to be this way."

Worries about the future are real fears. Sometimes the world appears to be spiraling out of control, especially if you tune in to a reputable news channel. Even scrolling through social media sometimes makes you feel like the world has lost its mind!

We don't have to fear the future. We may be concerned perhaps—and willing to do our part to make the world a better place. But the Bible tells us that God will never leave us—past, present, or future. God loves us, cares for us, and has good plans in mind.

When we cling to him daily, he empowers us to face whatever situation comes our way. When we walk in the light of his love, we have no reason to fear the darkness, whether in the present day or the future.

God goes before us, walks with us, and never ever leaves us. Let his presence dispel any fear of the future. He's got this!

- What about the future scares you? Is there something you can physically do to alleviate or abolish that fear? If the answer is yes, ask God to help you take action. If the answer is no, what will it take to give that fear completely to the Lord?
- Has someone ever abandoned you? Is that a current situation? What helps you get through the feelings of loss or betrayal? How can you believe with your mind and heart that God will never abandon you? Try repeating over and over: "God will never leave me nor forsake me."
- Close your eyes and thank God for taking care of you in the past. Thank him for being present with you now. And picture him going before you in very specific circumstances. Are you facing divorce? Picture God with you in the courtroom. Are adult children leaving the nest? Imagine him meeting you daily in your home. Facing financial issues? Picture him providing for your needs.

PRAYER

God, I'm so glad you never leave me. Thank
you for going before me. Amen.

Nothing Separates Us from God

For I am convinced that neither death nor life, neither angels nor demons, neither the present nor the future, nor any powers, neither height nor depth, nor anything else in all creation, will be able to separate us from the love of God that is in Christ Jesus our Lord.

ROMANS 8:38–39 (NIV)

After one and a half years of serving as his caregiver, Veronica lost her husband to pancreatic cancer when he was only 46. With one child in college and two in high school, Veronica struggled to make sense of her loss.

The loss of someone dear to us—through death or another circumstance that removes that person from our life—rocks our world and brings about a host of questions that most often begin with "Why?" And most of the time, answers never come in this lifetime. We can't understand why God allows certain tragedies and devastations.

Regardless, God is still good! He will always be good, despite our circumstances. Despite our lack of understanding. And nothing—no tragedy or death or devastating blow—*nothing* can separate us from God's love. He loved us before time began and will love us through all eternity.

God catches all of our tears. He understands our sadness. God is near to the brokenhearted, and he comforts us with his strength in ways that only he can. If you're grieving the loss of a loved one, reach for God. Lean into him and weep in the comfort of his loving arms.

REFLECTIONS

- Are you grieving the loss of someone important to you? Death, divorce, a change in foster care assignments, an empty nest, adult children moving far away, a broken relationship with a best friend—grief comes in many forms and can be really painful. What helps you cope with grief?
- Counselors often speak of the "stages of grief." Take some time to research each stage to help you realize you're not alone in your feelings. Who can you talk to about your grief? Who do you know who's been through the grief process and might be able to mentor you during this time?
- In what ways does it comfort you to know that nothing—NOTHING—can separate you from God's love? Death, sin, past mistakes, present situations, future cares—nothing at all can separate us from God's love. How can you remind yourself of that truth each day?

PRAYER

God, grief hurts. And it's hard. Please comfort me in my loss. Thank you for loving me with an everlasting love. Thank you for Jesus. Amen.

When Change Scares You, Trust the Unchanging Savior

Jesus Christ *is* the same yesterday, today, and forever.
HEBREWS 13:8 (NKJV)

When my husband announced he was joining the Navy, I balked at his decision. We'd almost completed our master's degrees, and I was teaching school just across the county line. Bottom line? Change frightened me. His job would require us to move away, and I was scared.

I begged God to modify David's plans, with never an added "Thy will be done" to my prayer. In the end, I moved reluctantly, but it wasn't long before I realized God's plans are always better than mine. You'd think I would have learned my lesson about facing changes by now, but I'll admit that I still struggle at times.

Change is inevitable in this world, but some of us handle it better than others. I'm so glad to know that the one true constant in life is my Savior and Lord. Jesus never changes. He is the same yesterday, today, tomorrow, and forever. We can hang on to that promise and truth. No matter where our ship takes us in life, Jesus will always be the same.

If you're switching jobs, changing careers completely, altering zip codes, moving into a new home, changing church homes, adding new family members, quitting your job to be a stay-at-home mom, starting a new degree—no matter what change you're facing in this season of life, know this for sure: Jesus Christ remains the same. Trust Him.

- What changes are you currently dealing with? How well do you handle change? Recall past changes. Were most of them good? Challenging? How did God see you through each one? How has God strengthened you to face new changes?
- Besides God of course, who helped you get through some of those life changes? How can you use what you learned during a past change to pay it forward and help someone else going through a similar situation?
- What is your favorite New Testament Bible story about Jesus? What character traits about Jesus captivate you the most? Compassionate? Servant-heart? Loving? Patient? Forgiving? What trait do you struggle to emulate? Which one comes easy for you? How can you help your kids strive to be more like Jesus? In what ways can you reassure them that Jesus remains the same always?

PRAYER

Jesus, I love you. In a life that's ever-changing, thank you for remaining the same, today, tomorrow, and forever. Thank you for dying on the cross for my sins. I'm enamored with your love for me. Amen.

Seen by the One Who Loves Me Most

Finally, be strong in the Lord and in his mighty power.
EPHESIANS 6:10 (NIV)

Meesha loved volunteering at the animal shelter. She actually liked mucking out canine stalls and never minded changing litter boxes, because she enjoyed interacting with the furry shelter residents in the process. She especially liked bathing the animals and sprucing them up, hoping the attention she gave them would make them more attractive and enhance their prospects for finding their new forever-homes.

"None of the paid employees seem to respect my opinions or sug-gestions," she told her husband one day after arriving home. "My love of God's creatures can't compare to their college degrees and years of experience. I just wish they'd listen to me occasionally."

Have you ever felt unseen? I certainly have. On some days, I've felt like my title was "just a mommy." Maybe that was a self-imposed title, but it felt real to me in light of others' words and actions.

You know what? Feeling unseen is hurtful, but God sees us and that's really all that matters. I love the verse in 2 Chronicles 16:9 (NIV) that begins, "For the eyes of the LORD range throughout the earth to strengthen those whose hearts are fully committed to him." God's eyes are forever on his children. There's never a time that God does not see you and me. He sees us; he loves us. I can be strong and confident, no matter who sees or doesn't see me, because my strength depends on God's mighty power and nothing else.

REFLECTIONS

- What's your favorite part about being a mom? Your least favorite? What parts of motherhood are most rewarding? How about most discouraging? When you look into the faces of your children, what comes to mind as the greatest joy of being their mom?
- When have you felt unseen? How can you best learn to trust that God sees you and not worry what others think, say, or do? Do you know a mom who feels overlooked? How can you help other moms and women feel seen and loved?
- In what ways does God give you strength? How does his power help you face the challenges of motherhood? How can you harness that power each morning to give you the strength you need to tackle every task that day? How can you remind yourself to lean into God's strength for every season of motherhood?

PRAYER

God, thank you for the gift of my precious children. Give me strength each day to raise them the way I should and to teach them to love you like I do. Remind me that you see and value me, always. Amen.

Strength for All Seasons of Motherhood

The LORD my Lord is my strength; he makes my feet like those of a deer and enables me to walk on mountain heights!

HABAKKUK 3:19 (CSB)

Brandi Lynne bravely quit her job as a receptionist and opened her own photography studio. She'd spent years honing her skills and wanted to spend more time with the family. With her husband's support and help, she could make her own hours and work around the kids' schedules.

"Weren't you nervous about starting something new?" her friend asked.

"Yes, but as they say, 'There's no time like the present,' and this is my gift to myself."

Have you thought about doing something new? A new job or career? Want to lead a Bible study for the first time? Begin a new hobby? Trust God and step into that new path with the Lord's strength and the sure-footed hooves of a deer! Climb new heights! Reach for the stars! Scale the mountaintops!

Trust God's promises and truth. Push back the darkness of self-doubt with the light of Jesus Christ. Hang on to God as you start down your new path. He is right there, by your side.

God offers strength in every season of motherhood. As a new mom—or as an experienced one. A young mom or a not-so-young one. Through changes, new experiences, disappointments, discouragements, challenges, mistakes and failures, fun times, adventures, accomplishments, successes, and so much more. God sees you. He is your stronghold and fortress in every way, in every season, in every minute. He will never leave you. God loves you immeasurably and forever. Let that love give you the confidence to boldly follow your path!

REFLECTIONS

- What new opportunity appeals to you? What dream would you like to see come true? What would it take from God to make either of those happen? Have you shared your dreams and aspirations with him? What would it take from you to see your dreams come to fruition? Are you willing to work toward that goal?
- In what areas of your life do you need God's strength the most? When have you "walked on mountain heights" because of God's strength? How and when have you shared those experiences with other moms who need to be empowered and inspired?
- What verses about God's strength and power have you memorized (or want to memorize) to help you during challenging mom-seasons? What steps can you take to draw closer to God and lean into his strength more deeply? How often do you thank God for strengthening you as a mom?

PRAYER

God, thank you for giving me strength in all seasons of motherhood. Thank you for inspiring me to try new things. You are so good to me, and I love you. Empower me, Lord, with your strength. Amen.

Resources

Here are two articles that offer grounding technique suggestions that can redirect your focus and distract you from an anxious feeling.

- mayoclinichealthsystem.org/hometown-health/speaking-of-health/5-4-3-2-1-countdown-to-make-anxiety-blast-off
- healthline.com/health/grounding-techniques

BOOKS

Make Up Your Mind: Unlock Your Thoughts, Transform Your Life by Denise Pass and Michelle Nietert

Fearless Women of the Bible: Finding Unshakable Confidence Despite Your Fears and Failures by Lynn Cowell

Before the Throne by Crickett Keeth

Refresh Your Hope by Lori Hatcher

Thirsty: 12 Weeks of Drinking Deeply from God's Word by Hannah C. Hall

They Call Me Mom: 52 Encouraging Devotions for Every Moment by Michelle Medlock Adams and Bethany Jett

Praying Through Every Emotion by Linda Evans Shepherd

The Third Path: Finding Intimacy with God on the Path of Questioning by Eva Marie Everson

Growing a Mother's Heart Bible Study by Karen Whiting

Soul Care When You're Weary by Edie Melson

Equipping Godly Women Podcast
equippinggodlywomen.com/podcast

Alli Worthington Show Podcast
alliworthington.com/topics/podcast

Risen Motherhood Podcast
risenmotherhood.com/podcast

Journeywomen Podcast
journeywomenpodcast.com

Grounded Podcast
reviveourhearts.com/podcast/grounded

Mental Health for Christian Women Podcast
podcasts.apple.com/us/podcast/mental-health-for-christian-women/
id1527510700

Therapy as a Christian Podcast
podcasts.apple.com/us/podcast/therapy-as-a-christian/id1443970723

Made For This with Jennie Allen Podcast
jennieallen.com/podcast

She Found Joy Podcast
shefoundjoy.com/resources/podcast

Don't Mom Alone with Heather MacFadyen Podcast
heathermacfadyen.com/podcast-show

WEBSITES

- courtnayerichard.com
- herviewfromhome.com
- christianitytoday.com/ct/topics/m/mental-health
- focusonthefamily.com/get-help/mental-health-resources
- channelmom.org

When you're looking for specific verses by topic:

- biblestudytools.com/topical-verses
- openbible.info/topics

Acknowledgments

To the four J's who made me a mommy: Jeremy, Jenifer, Jeb Daniel, and Jessica. You are my greatest treasures, and I love you all dearly! You are so precious, and words can never express how blessed I feel to be your mom. I thank God for you each day!

To our extra blessings, Adam and Dawson. We're so glad God added you to our family as sons-in-love. Thank you for being godly husbands and for taking such good care of our daughters.

To Benaiah (and other grandtreasures to come). Thank you for giving me the title of Grandmommy. I wear that hat proudly!

A special thanks to my husband, David. You're my biggest writing cheerleader, a wonderful husband and father, an amazing granddaddy, and my best friend forever. I wouldn't want to do this parenting job with anyone but you.

To our moms, Reta Bland and Karen Lavender. Thank you for teaching us what it means to be parents. We treasure our family trees and are very thankful for you.

To the hundreds of moms and grandmommies I've come to know and love over the years. Thank you for your wisdom, mentorship, encouragement, and love. It takes a community of moms to raise our kiddos, and I'm grateful for you all.

To my agent, Cyle Young. Thanks for everything!

To Penguin Random House. A huge thank you for another project that I've enjoyed immeasurably. I'm thankful for every person who helped this book become a reality. You're amazing!

Lastly, but first in my life, to my heavenly Father. *I've tasted and seen—YOU ARE GOOD!*

About the Author

Of all the hats **Julie Lavender** has worn, her favorite by far is the "mommy" hat. She believes it's the most challenging, yet most rewarding, position she's ever held. Julie thanks God every day for the gift of motherhood and is very grateful for God's blessings and guidance throughout her parenting journey.

An author, journalist, and former homeschooling mom of 25 years, Julie holds a master's degree in early childhood education. She is married to her high school and college sweetheart, and together, Julie and David are the parents of four, in-laws of two, and grandparents to a precious almost-five-year-old grandson.

Julie loved living in various locations across the country as the wife of a United States Navy medical entomologist. She taught public school before becoming a stay-at-home, homeschooling mommy. After her husband retired from active duty, the Lavenders moved back to their hometown, and David began work as a wildlife biologist at a nearby army installation.

Julie's most recent book, also published by Penguin Random House, *Children's Bible Stories for Bedtime*, was truly a heart-project, and Julie loves that the 52 Bible stories help children snuggle up with thoughts of God's love before going to bed each night. Prior to that, Julie wrote *365 Ways to Love Your Child: Turning Little Moments into Lasting Memories*, published by Revell/Baker, to encourage parents to show kids every day how much they are loved with simple but meaningful gestures and activities.

Learn more about Julie at JulieLavenderWrites.com and connect with her on social media. She loves getting to know other moms and grandmommies.